WHO'S
AMERICAN FOOTBALL

WHO'S WHO in AMERICAN FOOTBALL

KEN THOMAS
WITH NICK WRIDGWAY & ROGER SMITH

Macdonald
Queen Anne Press

In association with
Channel Four Television Company Limited

A **Queen Anne Press** BOOK

© by Ken Thomas 1986

First published in Great Britain in 1986 by Queen Anne Press, a
division of Macdonald & Co (Publishers) Ltd, Greater London
House, London NW1 7QX
A BPCC plc Company

Reprinted 1986

British Library Cataloguing in Publication Data
Thomas, Ken
    Who's who in American football.
    1. Football players—Biography
    I. Title II. Wridgway, Nick III. Smith, Roger
    796.332'092'2   GV939.A1

    ISBN 0-356-12814-8

Typeset by Solo Graphics.
Printed and bound in Great Britain by R.J. Acford, Chichester.

WALTER PAYTON

DAN FOUTS

INTRODUCTION

'He uses statistics like a drunken man uses lamp-posts — for support rather than illumination.'

And in that statement, by the late Andrew Lang, there is more than a grain of truth. No collection of figures can tell the whole story of a professional football player. Nonetheless, American Football is a game of gaining ground — and that precious commodity is measured in yardage. Not all players are paid to gain ground but some are, and the great offensive players gain lots of it. Furthermore, they do it with a frequency which sets them apart from mere mortals. This book lists the achievements of current NFL players, not only those who are great right now, but also those who might be even better tomorrow.

UNDERSTANDING THE NUMBERS

RUSHING

It's worth remembering that the offense has four downs in order to gain ten yards. In this light, then, an average gain per attempt of 4.0 yards is good. A player who averages 4.5 or more yards per carry is exceptionally good.

That's a basis from which to start but there is another factor to take into consideration, particularly, his number of carries per game (and of course per season). His average gain becomes significant, only when he has an appreciable number of carries per game. As a simple guideline, it's fair to assert that the figures begin to have meaning when the player rushes at least ten times per game. The major running backs will rush some 18 to 20 times a game, whilst the real workhorses might even top 25.

With these ideas in mind, let's now look at just what the average gain means (or might mean). An average of 5.0 certainly does not mean that the running back gains that number of yards every time he rushes. The following simple example will demonstrate the point.

Consider two running backs, A and B, each of whom has twenty rushes:

Player	Yards gained on each carry	Avg.
A	5 4 5 4 5 4 4 5 6 5 7 4 6 4 5 6 4 5 6 6	5.0
B	3 4 1 2 6 4 2 8 3 2 1 1 3 1 4 2 3 2 2 46	5.0

Player A is consistently good, gaining excellent yardage on every play.

Player B has a really tough time of it, working hard but gaining only poor yardage. But then he breaks for a long gain of 46 yards, bringing his average up to that of player A. The two are quite clearly different in style, and yet they end up with the same average.

The longest gain is a significant figure in interpreting the average gain, indeed, just a couple of big gains in a season can separate a player from the chasing pack. In addition, the 'longest gain' figure almost always indicates that the player has breakaway speed, and, usually, the ability to sidestep a defender in open-field play. Tony Dorsett is such a player, having registered gains of 99, 84, 77, 77, 75, 63 and 60 yards in a nine-year NFL career, over which he averages 4.4 yards per carry. Atlanta's William Andrews, on the other hand, is an entirely different kind of running back. His longest gain is 33 yards and yet, over his five-year career, he averages 4.6 yards per carry. In his way, he's just as valuable as Dorsett but, as the figures suggest, he's a punching, punishing runner, who can blast through the line of scrimmage but is easily caught by defenders. John Riggins, certainly over recent years, falls into the same category.

Looking at total yardage, the magic figures are 100 for a single game and 1,000 for a season. It is in those categories that the NFL lists its rushing records. In recent years, the value of the latter figure has come under question, particularly from those who would point out that there are now sixteen regular-season games, compared with the twelve when Jim Brown embarked on his sequence of eye-poppers. Still, even with the expanded season, it's only the thoroughbreds who break the four-figure barrier.

JOHN RIGGINS

DAN MARINO

PASSING AND PASS RECEIVING

Let's imagine a play on which the quarterback passes five yards to a receiver, who then goes on to gain another 75 yards before being stopped. The play has covered 80 yards. It would make sense to credit the passer with five yards and the receiver with 75. However, for statistical purposes, the NFL credits **both** players with an 80-yard gain. In a sense, by gaining yardage after the reception, the pass receiver is enhancing the passer's performance. But that's the way it is and there's not much point in arguing about it. Let's look firstly at passing.

PASSING

Over the years, for the purpose of identifying the individual Passing Champion, the NFL has used a variety of methods:

1932-1937   Total yards passing

1938-1940   Percentage of completions

1941-1948   There was an inverse ranking system based on the following
measures:-
Total completions
Percentage of completions
Total yards gained
Total touchdown passes
Number of interceptions
Percentage of interceptions

1949 only   As for 1941-1948 with the exclusion of 'Number of
interceptions'

1950-1959   Average yards gained per pass with a minimum of 100
attempts

1960-1961   There was an inverse ranking system based on the following
measures:- (minimum of ten attempts per game needed to
qualify)
Total completions
Total yards
Total touchdown passes
Percentage of completions
Percentage of interceptions
Average gain per attempt.

1962-1971   There was an inverse ranking system based on the following
measures:-
Percentage of completions
Total touchdown passes
Percentage of interceptions
Average gain per attempt

1972 only   As above but with the replacement of 'total touchdown
passes' by 'percentage of touchdown passes'

It was with a stroke of genius that, in 1973, the league adopted a system which includes just about everything that a passer does (or tries to do). It produces a figure known as the Passer Rating.

The official method involves the use of tables devised by the league's senior statisticians. However, there is an unofficial formula which can be used to calculate an accurate rating, providing that all the terms are expressed to two decimal figures. The formula is set out as follows:-

Rating = [comp.% + (avg. gain × 5) + 2.5 + (TD% × 4) − (Int.% × 5)] × 5/6

Completion Percentage (comp.%)	=	$\dfrac{\text{passes completed} \times 100}{\text{total passes attempted}}$
Average Gain (avg. gain)	=	$\dfrac{\text{yards gained}}{\text{total passes attempted}}$
Touchdown Percentage (TD%)	=	$\dfrac{\text{number of touchdowns} \times 100}{\text{total passes attempted}}$
Interception Percentage (Int.%)	=	$\dfrac{\text{number of interceptions} \times 100}{\text{total passes attempted}}$

(Note: A quarterback also rushes but this was excluded from the calculation – he is rated only on his performance as a passer.)

So what is a good passer rating? The maximum rating is 150*, and to achieve this the quarterback would have to equal the NFL single-season records in the above four categories. And not even Miami's Dan Marino is that good! A rating of more than 100 for a single season represents an astonishing performance, and he's a rattling good quarterback who can rate in the 80s. A figure in the high 90s would normally be good enough to win the league passing title.

*The vagaries of the system allow this to be exceeded but it happens only when a player throws a small number of passes. In this case, the rating is
meaningless.

PASS RECEIVING

All three groups of players, wide receivers, tight ends and running backs, catch passes. For the purposes of identifying the Passing Champion, the NFL uses 'number of receptions' and it is not unusual for the title to go to a running back or a tight end. However, in terms of 'yards receiving', the wide receivers normally lead the way. Also, the receivers will be some way ahead in terms of 'average gain', with the big-play specialists averaging more than 16.0 yards. Again, though, a low average need not indicate a lack of speed and may simply reflect that player's role in the offense. Take, for example, Pittsburgh's John Stallworth. Last year, his average was a modest 12.5 yards per reception and yet he is one of the league's deep threats. In his case, a low average would suggest that his job was to make those tough medium-range receptions, perhaps over the middle. Washington's Art Monk is another whose career average doesn't exactly set the alarm bells ringing. But here, too, it is more a reflection of his role as the man to whom the quarterback looks for the critical pass reception. New England's Stanley Morgan, on the other hand, is a burner. He is not prolific, in terms of pass receptions, but when he does catch the ball he's off like lightning. The tight ends would normally average somewhere around 12 yards per catch, but, remember, they often have to block an opposing player before moving out into position to make the reception. Running backs catch the short passes and normally average less than 10 yards per reception.

PLACEKICKING

It's worth remembering that the goalposts are sited on the end line, that is, ten yards beyond the goal line and it means that a field goal attempt, say from the 40-yard line, needs to travel 50 yards in order to be successful. It's a tough life for a placekicker in the NFL, especially if the offense is having a poor season. Time after time, the placekicker might be forced to attempt field goals from long range. Yet with a successful team, he might be given lots of close-range opportunities and, certainly, plenty of extra-point attempts. It is not necessarily true, then, that the kicker who scores the most points is the best. And there is the pressure factor. Attempting a field goal when your team is ahead by twenty points is a whole lot different from attempting the winning field goal, in the dying seconds of a game.

Accordingly, we make no claim that placekicking statistics, presented in this form, are particularly meaningful. Nonetheless, we felt that a list of players who've been notching 50-plus yarders over the years would be of some value.

ABERCROMBIE, Walter PITTSBURGH STEELERS
Position: Running Back; **Birthdate:** 26.09.59
College: Baylor; **Height:** 6–0; **Weight:** 210; **NFL Years:** 4

		RUSHING					RECEIVING				
Year	Club	Att.	Yds.	Avg.	Lg.	TDs	No.	Yds.	Avg.	Lg.	TDs
1982	Pittsburgh	21	100	4.8	34	2	1	14	14.0	14	0
1983	Pittsburgh	112	446	4.0	50t	4	26	391	15.0	51t	3
1984	Pittsburgh	145	610	4.2	31	1	16	135	8.4	59	0
1985	Pittsburgh	227	851	3.7	32t	7	24	209	8.7	27	2
Totals		**505**	**2,007**	**4.0**	**50t**	**14**	**67**	**749**	**11.2**	**59**	**5**

ADAMS, Curtis SAN DIEGO CHARGERS
Position: Running Back; **Birthdate:** 30.04.62
College: Central Michigan; **Height:** 5–11; **Weight:** 198; **NFL Years:** 1

		RUSHING					RECEIVING				
Year	Club	Att.	Yds.	Avg.	Lg.	TDs	No.	Yds.	Avg.	Lg.	TDs
1985	San Diego	16	49	3.1	14	1	1	12	12.0	12	0
Totals		**16**	**49**	**3.1**	**14**	**1**	**1**	**12**	**12.0**	**12**	**0**

ADAMS, George NEW YORK GIANTS
Position: Running Back; **Birthdate:** 22.12.62
College: Kentucky; **Height:** 6–1; **Weight:** 225; **NFL Years:** 1

		RUSHING					RECEIVING				
Year	Club	Att.	Yds.	Avg.	Lg.	TDs	No.	Yds.	Avg.	Lg.	TDs
1985	N.Y. Giants	128	498	3.9	39	2	31	389	12.5	70t	2
Totals		**128**	**498**	**3.9**	**39**	**2**	**31**	**389**	**12.5**	**70t**	**2**

ADAMS, Willis CLEVELAND BROWNS
Position: Wide Receiver – Tight End; **Birthdate:** 22.08.56
College: Houston; **Height:** 6–2; **Weight:** 200; **NFL Years:** 6

		RECEIVING				
Year	Club	No.	Yds.	Avg.	Lg.	TDs
1979	Cleveland	1	6	6.0	6	0
1980	Cleveland	8	165	20.6	39	0

Year	Club	No.	Yds.	Avg.	Lg.	TDs
1981	Cleveland	1	24	24.0	24	0
1982	Cleveland	0	0	0.0	0	0
1983	Cleveland	20	374	18.7	59	2
1984	Cleveland	21	261	12.4	24	0
1985	Cleveland	10	132	13.2	22	0
Totals		**61**	**962**	**15.8**	**59**	**2**

ALEXANDER, Charles CINCINNATI BENGALS
Position: Running Back; **Birthdate:** 28.07.57
College: Louisiana State; **Height:** 6–1; **Weight:** 226; **NFL Years:** 7

		RUSHING					RECEIVING				
Year	Club	Att.	Yds.	Avg.	Lg.	TDs	No.	Yds.	Avg.	Lg.	TDs
1979	Cincinnati	88	286	3.3	20	1	11	91	8.3	13	0
1980	Cincinnati	169	702	4.2	37	2	36	192	5.3	23	0
1981	Cincinnati	98	292	3.0	16	2	28	262	9.4	65t	1
1982	Cincinnati	64	207	3.2	18	1	14	85	6.1	14	1
1983	Cincinnati	153	523	3.4	12	3	32	187	5.8	14	0
1984	Cincinnati	132	479	3.6	22	2	29	203	7.0	22	0
1985	Cincinnati	44	156	3.5	18	2	15	110	7.3	19	0
Totals		**748**	**2,645**	**3.5**	**37**	**13**	**165**	**1,130**	**6.8**	**65t**	**2**

WALTER ABERCROMBIE

GEORGE ADAMS

15

ALLEGRE, Raul INDIANAPOLIS COLTS
Position: Placekicker; **Birthdate:** 15.06.59
College: Texas; **Height:** 5–10; **Weight:** 161; **NFL Years:** 3

		SCORING					
Year	Club	EPA	EPM	FGA	FGM	Lg.	Pts.
1983	Baltimore	24	22	35	30	55	112
1984	Indianapolis	14	14	18	11	54	47
1985	Indianapolis	39	36	26	16	41	84
Totals		**77**	**72**	**79**	**57**	**55**	**243**

ALLEN, Anthony ATLANTA FALCONS
Position: Wide Receiver; **Birthdate:** 29.06.59
College: Washington; **Height:** 5–11; **Weight:** 182; **NFL Years:** 1

		RECEIVING				
Year	Club	No.	Yds.	Avg.	Lg.	TDs
1985	Atlanta	14	207	14.8	37t	2
Totals		**14**	**207**	**14.8**	**37t**	**2**

ALLEN, Greg CLEVELAND BROWNS
Position: Running Back; **Birthdate:** 04.06.63
College: Florida State; **Height:** 5–11; **Weight:** 200; **NFL Years:** 1

		RUSHING					RECEIVING				
Year	Club	Att.	Yds.	Avg.	Lg.	TDs	No.	Yds.	Avg.	Lg.	TDs
1985	Cleveland	8	32	4.0	8	0	0	0	0.0	0	0
Totals		**8**	**32**	**4.0**	**8**	**0**	**0**	**0**	**0.0**	**0**	**0**

ALLEN, Marcus LOS ANGELES RAIDERS
Position: Running Back; **Birthdate:** 22.03.60
College: USC; **Height:** 6–2; **Weight:** 205; **NFL Years:** 4

		RUSHING					RECEIVING				
Year	Club	Att.	Yds.	Avg.	Lg.	TDs	No.	Yds.	Avg.	Lg.	TDs
1982	L.A. Raiders	160	697	4.4	53	11	38	401	10.6	51t	3
1983	L.A. Raiders	266	1,014	3.8	19	9	68	590	8.7	36	2

MARCUS ALLEN

MORTEN ANDERSEN

Year	Club	Att.	Yds.	Avg.	Lg.	TDs	No.	Yds.	Avg.	Lg.	TDs
1984	L.A. Raiders	275	1,168	4.2	52t	13	64	758	11.8	92	5
1985	L.A. Raiders	380	1,759	4.6	61t	11	67	555	8.3	44	3
Totals		**1,081**	**4,638**	**4.3**	**61t**	**44**	**237**	**2,304**	**9.7**	**92**	**13**

ANDERSEN, Morten NEW ORLEANS SAINTS
Position: Placekicker; **Birthdate:** 19.08.60
College: Michigan State; **Height:** 6–2; **Weight:** 205; **NFL Years:** 4

				SCORING			
Year	Club	EPA	EPM	FGA	FGM	Lg.	Pts.
1982	New Orleans	6	6	5	2	45	12
1983	New Orleans	38	37	24	18	52	91
1984	New Orleans	34	34	27	20	53	94
1985	New Orleans	29	27	35	31	55	120
Totals		**107**	**104**	**91**	**71**	**55**	**317**

ANDERSON, Alfred MINNESOTA VIKINGS
Position: Running Back; **Birthdate:** 04.08.61
College: Baylor; **Height:** 6–1; **Weight:** 213; **NFL Years:** 2

		RUSHING					RECEIVING				
Year	Club	Att.	Yds.	Avg.	Lg.	TDs	No.	Yds.	Avg.	Lg.	TDs
1984	Minnesota	201	773	3.8	23	2	17	102	6.0	28t	1
1985	Minnesota	50	121	2.4	10	4	16	175	10.9	54t	1
Totals		**251**	**894**	**3.6**	**23**	**6**	**33**	**277**	**8.4**	**54t**	**2**

GARY ANDERSON

KEN ANDERSON

ANDERSON, Brad CHICAGO BEARS
Position: Wide Receiver; **Birthdate:** 21.01.61
College: Arizona; **Height:** 6–2; **Weight:** 198; **NFL Years:** 2

		RECEIVING				
Year	Club	No.	Yds.	Avg.	Lg.	TDs
1984	Chicago	3	77	25.7	49t	1
1985	Chicago	1	6	6.0	6	0
Totals		**4**	**83**	**20.8**	**49t**	**1**

ANDERSON, Gary PITTSBURGH STEELERS
Position: Placekicker; **Birthdate:** 16.07.59
College: Syracuse; **Height:** 5–11; **Weight:** 170; **NFL Years:** 4

		SCORING					
Year	Club	EPA	EPM	FGA	FGM	Lg.	Pts.
1982	Pittsburgh	22	22	12	10	48	52
1983	Pittsburgh	39	38	31	27	49	119

Year	Club	EPA	EPM	FGA	FGM	Lg.	Pts.
1984	Pittsburgh	45	45	32	24	55	117
1985	Pittsburgh	40	40	42	33	52	139
Totals		**146**	**145**	**117**	**94**	**55**	**427**

ANDERSON, Gary SAN DIEGO CHARGERS
Position: Running Back; **Birthdate:** 18.04.61
College: Arkansas; **Height:** 6–0; **Weight:** 190; **NFL Years:** 1

		RUSHING					RECEIVING				
Year	Club	Att.	Yds.	Avg.	Lg.	TDs	No.	Yds.	Avg.	Lg.	TDs
1985	San Diego	116	429	3.7	27	4	35	422	12.1	52t	2
Totals		**116**	**429**	**3.7**	**27**	**4**	**35**	**422**	**12.1**	**52t**	**2**

ANDERSON, Ken CINCINNATI BENGALS
Position: Quarterback; **Birthdate:** 15.02.49
College: Augustana; **Height:** 6–3; **Weight:** 212; **NFL Years:** 15

		PASSING						
Year	Club	Att.	Comp.	Yds.	Lg.	TDs	Int.	Rat.
1971	Cincinnati	131	72	777	44t	5	4	72.4
1972	Cincinnati	301	171	1,918	65t	7	7	74.1
1973	Cincinnati	329	179	2,428	78t	18	12	81.5
1974	Cincinnati	328	213	2,667	77t	18	10	95.9
1975	Cincinnati	377	228	3,169	55	21	11	94.1
1976	Cincinnati	338	179	2,367	85t	19	14	77.0
1977	Cincinnati	323	166	2,145	94t	11	11	69.8
1978	Cincinnati	319	173	2,219	57	10	22	57.8
1979	Cincinnati	339	189	2,340	73t	16	10	80.9
1980	Cincinnati	275	166	1,778	67t	6	13	67.1
1981	Cincinnati	479	300	3,754	74t	29	10	98.5
1982	Cincinnati	309	218	2,495	56t	12	9	95.5
1983	Cincinnati	297	198	2,333	80t	12	13	85.6
1984	Cincinnati	275	175	2,107	80t	10	12	81.0
1985	Cincinnati	32	16	170	44t	2	0	86.7
Totals		**4,452**	**2,643**	**32,667**	**94t**	**196**	**158**	**82.0**

ANDERSON, Ottis ST. LOUIS CARDINALS
Position: Running Back; **Birthdate:** 19.01.57
College: Miami; **Height:** 6–2; **Weight:** 220; **NFL Years:** 7

| | | RUSHING | | | | | RECEIVING | | | | |
Year	Club	Att.	Yds.	Avg.	Lg.	TDs	No.	Yds.	Avg.	Lg.	TDs
1979	St. Louis	331	1,605	4.8	76t	8	41	308	7.5	28	2
1980	St. Louis	301	1,352	4.5	51t	9	36	308	8.6	35	0
1981	St. Louis	328	1,376	4.2	28	9	51	387	7.6	27	0
1982	St. Louis	145	587	4.0	64	3	14	106	7.6	19	0
1983	St. Louis	296	1,270	4.3	43	5	54	459	8.5	40	1
1984	St. Louis	289	1,174	4.1	24	6	70	611	8.7	57	2
1985	St. Louis	117	479	4.1	38	4	23	225	9.8	43	0
Totals		**1,807**	**7,843**	**4.3**	**76t**	**44**	**289**	**2,404**	**8.3**	**57**	**5**

OTTIS ANDERSON

DAVE ARCHER

ANDREWS, William ATLANTA FALCONS
Position: Running Back; **Birthdate:** 25.12.55
College: Auburn; **Height:** 6–0; **Weight:** 213; **NFL Years:** 5

		RUSHING					RECEIVING				
Year	Club	Att.	Yds.	Avg.	Lg.	TDs	No.	Yds.	Avg.	Lg.	TDs
1979	Atlanta	239	1,023	4.3	23	3	39	309	7.9	34	2
1980	Atlanta	265	1,308	4.9	33	4	51	456	8.9	26	1
1981	Atlanta	289	1,301	4.5	29	10	81	735	9.1	70t	2
1982	Atlanta	139	573	4.1	19t	5	42	503	12.0	86t	2
1983	Atlanta	331	1,567	4.7	27	7	59	609	10.3	40	4
1984	Atlanta					Did not play					
1985	Atlanta					Did not play					
Totals		**1,263**	**5,772**	**4.6**	**33**	**29**	**272**	**2,612**	**9.6**	**86t**	**11**

ANTHONY, Tyrone CHICAGO BEARS
Position: Running Back; **Birthdate:** 03.03.62
College: North Carolina; **Height:** 5–11; **Weight:** 212; **NFL Years:** 2

		RUSHING					RECEIVING				
Year	Club	Att.	Yds.	Avg.	Lg.	TDs	No.	Yds.	Avg.	Lg.	TDs
1984	New Orleans	20	105	5.3	19	1	12	113	9.4	32	0
1985	New Orleans	17	65	3.8	13	0	28	185	6.6	36	0
Totals		**37**	**170**	**4.6**	**19**	**1**	**40**	**298**	**7.5**	**36**	**0**

ARCHER, Dave ATLANTA FALCONS
Position: Quarterback; **Birthdate:** 15.02.62
College: Iowa State; **Height:** 6–2; **Weight:** 203; **NFL Years:** 2

		PASSING						
Year	Club	Att.	Comp.	Yds.	Lg.	TDs	Int.	Rat.
1984	Atlanta	18	11	181	34	1	1	90.3
1985	Atlanta	312	161	1,992	62t	7	17	56.5
Totals		**330**	**172**	**2,173**	**62t**	**8**	**18**	**58.3**

ARMSTRONG, Adger
Position: Running Back; **Birthdate:** 21.06.57
College: Texas A&M; **Height:** 6–0; **Weight:** 225; **NFL Years:** 6

		RUSHING					RECEIVING				
Year	Club	Att.	Yds.	Avg.	Lg.	TDs	No.	Yds.	Avg.	Lg.	TDs
1980	Houston	0	0	0.0	0	0	0	0	0.0	0	0
1981	Houston	31	146	4.7	18	0	29	278	9.6	48	1
1982	Houston	8	15	1.9	5	0	12	75	6.3	14	0
1983	Tampa Bay	7	30	4.3	7	0	15	173	11.5	41	2
1984	Tampa Bay	10	34	3.4	9	2	22	180	8.2	18	3
1985	Tampa Bay	2	6	3.0	8	0	2	4	2.0	3	1
Totals		**58**	**231**	**4.0**	**18**	**2**	**80**	**710**	**8.9**	**48**	**7**

ARNOLD, Walt KANSAS CITY CHIEFS
Position: Tight End; **Birthdate:** 31.08.58
College: New Mexico; **Height:** 6–3; **Weight:** 221; **NFL Years:** 6

		RECEIVING				
Year	Club	No.	Yds.	Avg.	Lg.	TDs
1980	L.A. Rams	5	75	15.0	33	1
1981	L.A. Rams	20	212	10.6	24	2
1982	Houston	0	0	0.0	0	0
1983	Houston	12	137	11.4	37	1
1984	Wash.–K.C.	11	95	8.6	15	1
1985	Kansas City	28	339	12.1	38	1
Totals		**76**	**858**	**11.3**	**38**	**6**

AUSTIN, Cliff ATLANTA FALCONS
Position: Running Back; **Birthdate:** 02.03.60
College: Clemson; **Height:** 6–0; **Weight:** 207; **NFL Years:** 3

		RUSHING					RECEIVING				
Year	Club	Att.	Yds.	Avg.	Lg.	TDs	No.	Yds.	Avg.	Lg.	TDs
1983	New Orleans	4	16	4.0	5	0	2	25	12.5	18	0
1984	Atlanta	4	7	1.8	3	0	0	0	0.0	0	0
1985	Atlanta	20	110	5.5	17	0	1	21	21.0	21	0
Totals		**28**	**133**	**4.8**	**17**	**0**	**3**	**46**	**15.3**	**21**	**0**

BAHR, Chris LOS ANGELES RAIDERS
Position: Placekicker; **Birthdate:** 03.02.53
College: Penn State; **Height:** 5–10; **Weight:** 170; **NFL Years:** 10

		SCORING					
Year	Club	EPA	EPM	FGA	FGM	Lg.	Pts.
1976	Cincinnati	42	39	27	14	51	81
1977	Cincinnati	26	25	27	19	48	82
1978	Cincinnati	29	26	30	16	52	74
1979	Cincinnati	42	40	23	13	55	79
1980	Oakland	44	41	37	19	48	98
1981	Oakland	33	27	24	14	51	69
1982	L.A. Raiders	33	32	16	10	43	62
1983	L.A. Raiders	53	51	27	21	47	114
1984	L.A. Raiders	42	40	27	20	50	100
1985	L.A. Raiders	42	40	32	20	51	100
Totals		**386**	**361**	**270**	**166**	**55**	**859**

ADGER ARMSTRONG

CHRIS BAHR

BAHR, Matt CLEVELAND BROWNS
Position: Placekicker; **Birthdate:** 06.07.56
College: Penn State; **Height:** 5–10; **Weight:** 175; **NFL Years:** 7

				SCORING			
Year	**Club**	**EPA**	**EPM**	**FGA**	**FGM**	**Lg.**	**Pts.**
1979	Pittsburgh	52	50	30	18	47	104
1980	Pittsburgh	42	39	28	19	48	96
1981	S.F.-Cle.	34	34	26	15	47	79
1982	Cleveland	17	17	15	7	46	38
1983	Cleveland	40	38	24	21	47	101
1984	Cleveland	25	25	32	24	50	97
1985	Cleveland	35	35	18	14	45	77
Totals		**245**	**238**	**173**	**118**	**50**	**592**

STACEY BAILEY

FRED BANKS

BAILEY, Stacey ATLANTA FALCONS
Position: Wide Receiver; **Birthdate:** 10.02.60
College: San Jose State; **Height:** 6–0; **Weight:** 157; **NFL Years:** 4

		RECEIVING				
Year	**Club**	**No.**	**Yds.**	**Avg.**	**Lg.**	**TDs**
1982	Atlanta	2	24	12.0	15	1
1983	Atlanta	55	881	16.0	53	6
1984	Atlanta	67	1,138	17.0	61	6
1985	Atlanta	30	364	12.1	31	0
Totals		**154**	**2,407**	**15.6**	**61**	**13**

BANKS, Fred CLEVELAND BROWNS
Position: Wide Receiver; **Birthdate:** 26.05.62
College: Liberty University; **Height:** 5–10; **Weight:** 177; **NFL Years:** 1

		RECEIVING				
Year	**Club**	**No.**	**Yds.**	**Avg.**	**Lg.**	**TDs**
1985	Cleveland	5	62	12.4	17t	2
Totals		**5**	**62**	**12.4**	**17t**	**2**

BARBER, Marion NEW YORK JETS
Position: Running Back; **Birthdate:** 06.12.59
College: Minnesota; **Height:** 6–2; **Weight:** 224; **NFL Years:** 4

		RUSHING					RECEIVING				
Year	**Club**	**Att.**	**Yds.**	**Avg.**	**Lg.**	**TDs**	**No.**	**Yds.**	**Avg.**	**Lg.**	**TDs**
1981	N.Y. Jets					Did not play					
1982	N.Y. Jets	8	24	3.0	4	0	0	0	0.0	0	0
1983	N.Y. Jets	15	77	5.1	13	1	7	48	6.9	12	1
1984	N.Y. Jets	31	148	4.8	18	2	10	79	7.9	17	0
1985	N.Y. Jets	9	41	4.6	10	0	3	46	15.3	22	0
Totals		**63**	**290**	**4.6**	**18**	**3**	**20**	**173**	**8.7**	**22**	**1**

BARBER, Mike DENVER BRONCOS
Position: Tight End; **Birthdate:** 04.06.53
College: Louisiana Tech; **Height:** 6–3; **Weight:** 237; **NFL Years:** 9

		RECEIVING				
Year	Club	No.	Yds.	Avg.	Lg.	TDs
1976	Houston	0	0	0.0	0	0
1977	Houston	9	94	10.4	23	1
1978	Houston	32	513	16.0	72t	3
1979	Houston	27	377	14.0	37t	3
1980	Houston	59	712	12.1	79t	5
1981	Houston	13	190	14.6	35	1
1982	L.A. Rams	18	166	9.2	21	1
1983	L.A. Rams	55	657	11.9	42t	3
1984	L.A. Rams	7	42	6.0	11	0
1985	L.A.–Denver	2	37	18.5	29	0
Totals		**222**	**2,788**	**12.6**	**79t**	**17**

BARTKOWSKI, Steve LOS ANGELES RAMS
Position: Quarterback; **Birthdate:** 12.11.52
College: California; **Height:** 6–4; **Weight:** 218; **NFL Years:** 11

		PASSING						
Year	Club	Att.	Comp.	Yds.	Lg.	TDs	Int.	Rat.
1975	Atlanta	255	115	1,662	68	13	15	59.3
1976	Atlanta	120	57	677	50t	2	9	39.6
1977	Atlanta	136	64	796	73t	5	13	38.5
1978	Atlanta	369	187	2,489	71	10	18	61.1
1979	Atlanta	380	204	2,505	57	17	20	67.2
1980	Atlanta	463	257	3,544	81t	31	16	88.0
1981	Atlanta	533	297	3,829	70t	30	23	79.2
1982	Atlanta	262	166	1,905	86t	8	11	78.1
1983	Atlanta	432	274	3,167	76t	22	5	97.6
1984	Atlanta	269	181	2,158	61	11	10	89.7
1985	Atl.-Washington	111	69	738	62t	5	1	92.8
Totals		**3,330**	**1,871**	**23,470**	**86t**	**154**	**141**	**76.0**

BASCHNAGEL, Brian CHICAGO BEARS
Position: Wide Receiver; **Birthdate:** 08.01.54
College: Ohio State; **Height:** 6–0; **Weight:** 184; **NFL Years:** 9

		RECEIVING				
Year	Club	No.	Yds.	Avg.	Lg.	TDs
1976	Chicago	13	226	17.4	58	0
1977	Chicago	4	50	12.5	25	0
1978	Chicago	2	29	14.5	22	0
1979	Chicago	30	452	15.1	54t	2
1980	Chicago	28	396	14.1	37	2
1981	Chicago	34	554	16.3	72t	3
1982	Chicago	12	194	16.2	39t	2
1983	Chicago	5	70	14.0	24	0
1984	Chicago	6	53	8.8	17	0
1985	Chicago			Did not play		
Totals		**134**	**2,024**	**15.1**	**72t**	**9**

STEVE BARTKOWSKI

MARK BAVARO

27

GREG BELL

JERRY BELL

BAVARO, Mark NEW YORK GIANTS
Position: Tight End; **Birthdate:** 28.04.63
College: Notre Dame; **Height:** 6–4; **Weight:** 245; **NFL Years:** 1

				RECEIVING		
Year	Club	No.	Yds.	Avg.	Lg.	TDs
1985	N.Y. Giants	37	511	13.8	32	4
Totals		**37**	**511**	**13.8**	**32**	**4**

BEACH, Pat INDIANAPOLIS COLTS
Position: Tight End; **Birthdate:** 28.12.59
College: Washington State; **Height:** 6–4; **Weight:** 242; **NFL Years:** 3

				RECEIVING		
Year	Club	No.	Yds.	Avg.	Lg.	TDs
1982	Baltimore	4	45	11.3	17	1
1983	Baltimore	5	56	11.2	16	1
1984	Indianapolis			Did not play		
1985	Indianapolis	36	376	10.4	30	6
Totals		**45**	**477**	**10.6**	**30**	**8**

BELL, Greg BUFFALO BILLS
Position: Running Back; **Birthdate:** 01.08.62
College: Notre Dame; **Height:** 5–10; **Weight:** 210; **NFL Years:** 2

Year	Club	RUSHING					RECEIVING				
		Att.	Yds.	Avg.	Lg.	TDs	No.	Yds.	Avg.	Lg.	TDs
1984	Buffalo	262	1,100	4.2	85t	7	34	277	8.1	37	1
1985	Buffalo	223	883	4.0	77t	8	58	576	9.9	49	1
Totals		**485**	**1,983**	**4.1**	**85t**	**15**	**92**	**853**	**9.3**	**49**	**2**

BELL, Jerry TAMPA BAY BUCCANEERS
Position: Tight End; **Birthdate:** 07.03.59
College: Arizona State; **Height:** 6–5; **Weight:** 230; **NFL Years:** 4

Year	Club	RECEIVING				
		No.	Yds.	Avg.	Lg.	TDs
1982	Tampa Bay	1	5	5.0	5	0
1983	Tampa Bay	18	200	11.1	33	1
1984	Tampa Bay	29	397	13.7	27	4
1985	Tampa Bay	43	496	11.5	27	2
Totals		**91**	**1,098**	**12.1**	**33**	**7**

BELL, Theo TAMPA BAY BUCCANEERS
Position: Wide Receiver; **Birthdate:** 21.12.53
College: Arizona; **Height:** 6–0; **Weight:** 190; **NFL Years:** 9

Year	Club	RECEIVING				
		No.	Yds.	Avg.	Lg.	TDs
1976	Pittsburgh	3	43	14.3	19	1
1977	Pittsburgh			Did not play		
1978	Pittsburgh	6	53	8.8	15t	1
1979	Pittsburgh	3	61	20.3	31	0
1980	Pittsburgh	29	748	25.8	72	2
1981	Tampa Bay	21	318	15.1	58t	2
1982	Tampa Bay	15	203	13.5	25	0
1983	Tampa Bay	25	410	16.4	52	2
1984	Tampa Bay	22	350	15.9	29	0
1985	Tampa Bay	12	189	15.8	24	0
Totals		**136**	**2,375**	**17.5**	**72**	**8**

BENDROSS, Jesse TAMPA BAY BUCCANEERS
Position: Wide Receiver; **Birthdate:** 19.05.61
College: Alabama; **Height:** 6–0; **Weight:** 200; **NFL Years:** 2

		RECEIVING				
Year	**Club**	**No.**	**Yds.**	**Avg.**	**Lg.**	**TDs**
1984	San Diego	16	213	13.3	29	0
1985	San Diego	11	156	14.2	54t	2
Totals		**27**	**369**	**13.7**	**54t**	**2**

BENIRSCHKE, Rolf SAN DIEGO CHARGERS
Position: Placekicker; **Birthdate:** 07.02.55
College: California-Davis; **Height:** 6–1; **Weight:** 183; **NFL Years:** 8

		SCORING					
Year	**Club**	**EPA**	**EPM**	**FGA**	**FGM**	**Lg.**	**Pts.**
1977	San Diego	25	21	23	17	47	72
1978	San Diego	43	37	22	18	44	91
1979	San Diego	13	12	4	4	42	24
1980	San Diego	48	46	36	24	53	118
1981	San Diego	61	55	26	19	52	112
1982	San Diego	34	32	22	16	51	80

WOODY BENNETT

CLIFF BENSON

Year	Club	EPA	EPM	FGA	FGM	Lg.	Pts.
1983	San Diego	45	43	24	15	51	88
1984	San Diego	41	41	26	17	51	92
1985	San Diego	2	2	0	0	00	2
Totals		**314**	**289**	**184**	**130**	**53**	**679**

BENNETT, Woody MIAMI DOLPHINS
Position: Running Back; **Birthdate:** 24.03.55
College: Miami; **Height:** 6–2; **Weight:** 225; **NFL Years:** 7

		RUSHING					RECEIVING			
Year	Club	Att.	Yds.	Avg.	Lg.	TDs	No.	Yds.	Avg.	Lg.	TDs
1979	N.Y. Jets	2	4	2.0	3	1	1	9	9.0	9	0
1980	N.Y. J-Miami	46	200	4.3	19	0	3	26	8.7	19t	1
1981	Miami	28	104	3.7	12	0	4	22	5.5	10	0
1982	Miami	9	15	1.7	5	0	0	0	0.0	0	0
1983	Miami	49	197	4.0	25	2	6	35	5.8	9	0
1984	Miami	144	606	4.2	23	7	6	44	7.3	20	1
1985	Miami	54	256	4.7	17	0	10	101	10.1	27t	1
Totals		**332**	**1,382**	**4.2**	**25**	**10**	**30**	**237**	**7.9**	**27t**	**3**

BENSON, Cliff ATLANTA FALCONS
Position: Tight End; **Birthdate:** 28.08.61
College: Purdue; **Height:** 6–4; **Weight:** 238; **NFL Years:** 2

		RECEIVING			
Year	Club	No.	Yds.	Avg.	Lg.	TDs
1984	Atlanta	26	244	9.4	30	0
1985	Atlanta	10	37	3.7	6	0
Totals		**36**	**281**	**7.8**	**30**	**0**

BENTLEY, Albert INDIANAPOLIS COLTS
Position: Running Back; **Birthdate:** 15.08.60
College: Miami; **Height:** 5–11; **Weight:** 207; **NFL Years:** 1

		RUSHING					RECEIVING			
Year	Club	Att.	Yds.	Avg.	Lg.	TDs	No.	Yds.	Avg.	Lg.	TDs
1985	Indianapolis	54	288	5.3	26t	2	11	85	7.7	16	0
Totals		**54**	**288**	**5.3**	**26t**	**2**	**11**	**85**	**7.7**	**16**	**0**

BLACKLEDGE, Todd KANSAS CITY CHIEFS
Position: Quarterback; **Birthdate:** 25.02.61
College: Penn State; **Height:** 6–3; **Weight:** 225; **NFL Years:** 3

		PASSING						
Year	Club	Att.	Comp.	Yds.	Lg.	TDs	Int.	Rat.
1983	Kansas City	34	20	259	43	3	0	112.3
1984	Kansas City	294	147	1,707	46t	6	11	59.2
1985	Kansas City	172	86	1,190	70t	6	14	50.3
Totals		**500**	**253**	**3,156**	**70t**	**15**	**25**	**59.7**

BLAND, Carl DETROIT LIONS
Position: Wide Receiver; **Birthdate:** 17.08.61
College: Virginia Union; **Height:** 5–11; **Weight:** 182; **NFL Years:** 2

		RECEIVING				
Year	Club	No.	Yds.	Avg.	Lg.	TDs
1984	Detroit	0	0	0.0	0	0
1985	Detroit	12	157	13.1	24	0
Totals		**12**	**157**	**13.1**	**24**	**0**

BLIGEN, Dennis NEW YORK JETS
Position: Running Back; **Birthdate:** 03.03.62
College: St. John's; **Height:** 5–11; **Weight:** 209; **NFL Years:** 2

		RUSHING					RECEIVING				
Year	Club	Att.	Yds.	Avg.	Lg.	TDs	No.	Yds.	Avg.	Lg.	TDs
1984	N.Y. Jets	0	0	0.0	0	0	0	0	0.0	0	0
1985	N.Y. Jets	22	107	4.9	28t	1	5	43	8.6	14	0
Totals		**22**	**107**	**4.9**	**28t**	**1**	**5**	**43**	**8.6**	**14**	**0**

BOJOVIC, Novo
Position: Placekicker; **Birthdate:** 02.11.59
College: Central Michigan; **Height:** 5–10; **Weight:** 170; **NFL Years:** 1

		SCORING					
Year	Club	EPA	EPM	FGA	FGM	Lg.	Pts.
1985	St. Louis	12	11	7	3	42	20
Totals		**12**	**11**	**7**	**3**	**42**	**20**

BOUZA, Matt INDIANAPOLIS COLTS
Position: Wide Receiver; **Birthdate:** 08.04.59
College: California; **Height:** 6–3; **Weight:** 212; **NFL Years:** 4

		RECEIVING				
Year	Club	No.	Yds.	Avg.	Lg.	TDs
1981	San Francisco	0	0	0.0	0	0
1982	Baltimore	22	287	13.0	34	2
1983	Baltimore	25	385	15.4	26	0
1984	Indianapolis	22	270	12.3	22	0
1985	Indianapolis	27	381	14.1	40	2
Totals		**96**	**1,323**	**13.8**	**40**	**4**

BOYER, Mark INDIANAPOLIS COLTS
Position: Tight End; **Birthdate:** 16.09.62
College: USC; **Height:** 6–4; **Weight:** 233; **NFL Years:** 1

		RECEIVING				
Year	Club	No.	Yds.	Avg.	Lg.	TDs
1985	Indianapolis	25	274	11.0	33	0
Totals		**25**	**274**	**11.0**	**33**	**0**

TODD BLACKLEDGE

MATT BOUZA

33

BRANCH, Cliff LOS ANGELES RAIDERS
Position: Wide Receiver; **Birthdate:** 01.08.48
College: Colorado; **Height:** 5–11; **Weight:** 170; **NFL Years:** 14

		RECEIVING				
Year	Club	No.	Yds.	Avg.	Lg.	TDs
1972	Oakland	3	41	13.7	19	0
1973	Oakland	19	290	15.3	53	3
1974	Oakland	60	1,092	18.2	67t	13
1975	Oakland	51	893	17.5	53t	9
1976	Oakland	46	1,111	24.2	88t	12
1977	Oakland	33	540	16.4	43	6
1978	Oakland	49	709	14.5	41	1
1979	Oakland	59	844	14.3	66t	6
1980	Oakland	44	858	19.5	86t	7
1981	Oakland	41	635	15.5	53	1
1982	L.A. Raiders	30	575	19.2	51	4
1983	L.A. Raiders	39	696	17.8	99t	5
1984	L.A. Raiders	27	401	14.9	47	0
1985	L.A. Raiders	0	0	0.0	0	0
Totals		**501**	**8,685**	**17.3**	**99t**	**67**

BREECH, Jim CINCINNATI BENGALS
Position: Placekicker; **Birthdate:** 11.04.56
College: California; **Height:** 5–6; **Weight:** 161; **NFL Years:** 7

		SCORING					
Year	Club	EPA	EPM	FGA	FGM	Lg.	Pts.
1978	Oakland	0	0	0	0	00	0
1979	Oakland	45	41	27	18	47	95
1980	Cincinnati	12	11	7	4	42	23
1981	Cincinnati	51	49	32	22	51	115
1982	Cincinnati	26	25	18	14	50	67
1983	Cincinnati	41	39	23	16	47	87
1984	Cincinnati	37	37	31	22	48	103
1985	Cincinnati	50	48	33	24	53	120
Totals		**262**	**250**	**171**	**120**	**53**	**610**

CLIFF BRANCH

HOBY BRENNER

BRENNAN, Brian CLEVELAND BROWNS
Position: Wide Receiver; **Birthdate:** 15.02.62
College: Boston College; **Height:** 5–9; **Weight:** 178; **NFL Years:** 2

		RECEIVING				
Year	**Club**	**No.**	**Yds.**	**Avg.**	**Lg.**	**TDs**
1984	Cleveland	35	455	13.0	52	3
1985	Cleveland	32	487	15.2	57	0
Totals		**67**	**942**	**14.1**	**57**	**3**

BRENNER, Hoby NEW ORLEANS SAINTS
Position: Tight End; **Birthdate:** 02.06.59
College: USC; **Height:** 6–4; **Weight:** 245; **NFL Years:** 5

		RECEIVING				
Year	**Club**	**No.**	**Yds.**	**Avg.**	**Lg.**	**TDs**
1981	New Orleans	7	143	20.4	34	0
1982	New Orleans	16	171	10.7	25	0
1983	New Orleans	41	574	14.0	38t	3
1984	New Orleans	28	554	19.8	57	6
1985	New Orleans	42	652	15.5	30	3
Totals		**134**	**2,094**	**15.6**	**57**	**12**

BRIGHT, Leon TAMPA BAY BUCCANEERS
Position: Running Back; **Birthdate:** 19.05.55
College: Florida State; **Height:** 5–9; **Weight:** 200; **NFL Years:** 5

		RUSHING					RECEIVING				
Year	Club	Att.	Yds.	Avg.	Lg.	TDs	No.	Yds.	Avg.	Lg.	TDs
1981	N.Y. Giants	51	197	3.9	25	2	28	291	10.4	36	0
1982	N.Y. Giants	1	5	5.0	5	0	2	19	9.5	13	0
1983	N.Y. Giants	1	2	2.0	2	0	2	33	16.5	19	0
1984	Tampa Bay	0	0	0.0	0	0	0	0	0.0	0	0
1985	Tampa Bay	0	0	0.0	0	0	0	0	0.0	0	0
Totals		**53**	**204**	**3.8**	**25**	**2**	**32**	**343**	**10.7**	**36**	**0**

BROCK, Dieter LOS ANGELES RAMS
Position: Quarterback; **Birthdate:** 12.02.51
College: Jacksonville State; **Height:** 6–0; **Weight:** 195; **NFL Years:** 1

		PASSING						
Year	Club	Att.	Comp.	Yds.	Lg.	TDs	Int.	Rat.
1985	L.A. Rams	365	218	2,658	64t	16	13	82.0
Totals		**365**	**218**	**2,658**	**64t**	**16**	**13**	**82.0**

JAMES BROOKS

CHARLIE BROWN

BROOKINS, Mitchell BUFFALO BILLS
Position: Wide Receiver; **Birthdate:** 10.12.60
College: Illinois; **Height:** 5–11; **Weight:** 196; **NFL Years:** 2

		RECEIVING				
Year	Club	No.	Yds.	Avg.	Lg.	TDs
1984	Buffalo	18	318	17.7	70t	1
1985	Buffalo	3	71	23.7	46	0
Totals		**21**	**389**	**18.5**	**70t**	**1**

BROOKS, James CINCINNATI BENGALS
Position: Running Back; **Birthdate:** 28.12.58
College: Auburn; **Height:** 5–10; **Weight:** 182; **NFL Years:** 5

		RUSHING					RECEIVING				
Year	Club	Att.	Yds.	Avg.	Lg.	TDs	No.	Yds.	Avg.	Lg.	TDs
1981	San Diego	109	525	4.8	28t	3	46	329	7.2	29t	3
1982	San Diego	87	430	4.9	48t	6	13	66	5.1	12	0
1983	San Diego	127	516	4.1	61	3	25	215	8.6	36	0
1984	Cincinnati	103	396	3.8	33	2	34	268	7.9	27t	2
1985	Cincinnati	192	929	4.8	39	7	55	576	10.5	57t	5
Totals		**618**	**2,796**	**4.5**	**61**	**21**	**173**	**1,454**	**8.4**	**57t**	**10**

BROWN, Charlie ATLANTA FALCONS
Position: Wide Receiver; **Birthdate:** 29.10.58
College: South Carolina State; **Height:** 5–10; **Weight:** 184; **NFL Years:** 4

		RECEIVING				
Year	Club	No.	Yds.	Avg.	Lg.	TDs
1981	Washington			Did not play		
1982	Washington	32	690	21.6	78t	8
1983	Washington	78	1,225	15.7	75t	8
1984	Washington	18	200	11.1	36	3
1985	Atlanta	24	412	17.2	48	2
Totals		**152**	**2,527**	**16.6**	**78t**	**21**

EDDIE BROWN

TED BROWN

BROWN, Eddie CINCINNATI BENGALS
Position: Wide Receiver; **Birthdate:** 17.12.62
College: Miami; **Height:** 6–0; **Weight:** 185; **NFL Years:** 1

		RECEIVING				
Year	Club	No.	Yds.	Avg.	Lg.	TDs
1985	Cincinnati	53	942	17.8	68t	8
Totals		**53**	**942**	**17.8**	**68t**	**8**

BROWN, Ron LOS ANGELES RAMS
Position: Wide Receiver; **Birthdate:** 31.03.61
College: Arizona State; **Height:** 5–11; **Weight:** 181; **NFL Years:** 2

		RECEIVING				
Year	Club	No.	Yds.	Avg.	Lg.	TDs
1984	L.A. Rams	23	478	20.8	54	4
1985	L.A. Rams	14	215	15.4	43t	3
Totals		**37**	**693**	**18.7**	**54**	**7**

BROWN, Ted MINNESOTA VIKINGS
Position: Running Back; **Birthdate:** 02.02.57
College: North Carolina State; **Height:** 5–10; **Weight:** 206; **NFL Years:** 7

		RUSHING					RECEIVING				
Year	**Club**	**Att.**	**Yds.**	**Avg.**	**Lg.**	**TDs**	**No.**	**Yds.**	**Avg.**	**Lg.**	**TDs**
1979	Minnesota	130	551	4.2	34	1	31	197	6.4	35	0
1980	Minnesota	219	912	4.2	55t	8	62	623	10.0	67t	2
1981	Minnesota	274	1,063	3.9	34	6	83	694	8.4	63	2
1982	Minnesota	120	515	4.3	30	1	31	207	6.7	29	2
1983	Minnesota	120	476	4.0	43	10	41	357	8.7	25	1
1984	Minnesota	98	442	4.5	19	3	46	349	7.6	35	3
1985	Minnesota	93	336	3.6	30	7	30	291	9.7	54t	3
Totals		**1,054**	**4,295**	**4.1**	**55t**	**36**	**324**	**2,718**	**8.4**	**67t**	**13**

BRUNNER, Scott ST. LOUIS CARDINALS
Position: Quarterback; **Birthdate:** 24.03.57
College: Delaware; **Height:** 6–5; **Weight:** 200; **NFL Years:** 5

		PASSING						
Year	**Club**	**Att.**	**Comp.**	**Yds.**	**Lg.**	**TDs**	**Int.**	**Rat.**
1980	N.Y. Giants	112	52	610	50t	4	6	53.0
1981	N.Y. Giants	190	79	978	43	5	11	42.7
1982	N.Y. Giants	298	161	2,017	47	10	9	74.1
1983	N.Y. Giants	386	190	2,516	62	9	22	54.3
1984	Denver			Did not play				
1985	St. Louis	60	30	336	40t	1	6	33.1
Totals		**1,046**	**512**	**6,457**	**62**	**29**	**54**	**56.3**

BURKETT, Chris BUFFALO BILLS
Position: Wide Receiver; **Birthdate:** 23.08.62
College: Jackson State; **Height:** 6–4; **Weight:** 198; **NFL Years:** 1

		RECEIVING				
Year	**Club**	**No.**	**Yds.**	**Avg.**	**Lg.**	**TDs**
1985	Buffalo	21	371	17.7	38	0
Totals		**21**	**371**	**17.7**	**38**	**0**

BUTLER, Jerry BUFFALO BILLS
Position: Wide Receiver; **Birthdate:** 12.10.57
College: Clemson; **Height:** 6–0; **Weight:** 178; **NFL Years:** 6

		RECEIVING				
Year	Club	No.	Yds.	Avg.	Lg.	TDs
1979	Buffalo	48	834	17.4	75t	4
1980	Buffalo	57	832	14.6	69	6
1981	Buffalo	55	842	15.3	67t	8
1982	Buffalo	26	336	12.9	47	4
1983	Buffalo	36	385	10.7	25	3
1984	Buffalo			Did not play		
1985	Buffalo	41	770	18.8	60t	2
Totals		**263**	**3,999**	**15.2**	**75t**	**27**

BUTLER, Kevin CHICAGO BEARS
Position: Placekicker; **Birthdate:** 24.07.62
College: Georgia; **Height:** 6–1; **Weight:** 204; **NFL Years:** 1

		SCORING					
Year	Club	EPA	EPM	FGA	FGM	Lg.	Pts.
1985	Chicago	51	51	37	31	46	144
Totals		**51**	**51**	**37**	**31**	**46**	**144**

BUTLER, Ray SEATTLE SEAHAWKS
Position: Wide Receiver; **Birthdate:** 28.06.56
College: USC; **Height:** 6–3; **Weight:** 197; **NFL Years:** 6

		RECEIVING				
Year	Club	No.	Yds.	Avg.	Lg.	TDs
1980	Baltimore	34	574	16.9	42	2
1981	Baltimore	46	832	18.1	67t	9
1982	Baltimore	17	268	15.8	53t	2
1983	Baltimore	10	207	20.7	60	3
1984	Indianapolis	43	664	15.4	74t	6
1985	Ind.–Seattle	19	345	18.2	72t	2
Totals		**169**	**2,890**	**17.1**	**74t**	**24**

BYNER, Earnest CLEVELAND BROWNS
Position: Running Back; **Birthdate:** 15.09.62
College: East Carolina; **Height:** 5–10; **Weight:** 215; **NFL Years:** 2

Year	Club	RUSHING					RECEIVING				
		Att.	Yds.	Avg.	Lg.	TDs	No.	Yds.	Avg.	Lg.	TDs
1984	Cleveland	72	426	5.9	54	2	11	118	10.7	26	0
1985	Cleveland	244	1,002	4.1	36	8	45	460	10.2	31	2
Totals		**316**	**1,428**	**4.5**	**54**	**10**	**56**	**578**	**10.3**	**31**	**2**

CAMPBELL, Earl NEW ORLEANS SAINTS
Position: Running Back; **Birthdate:** 29.03.55
College: Texas; **Height:** 5–11; **Weight:** 233; **NFL Years:** 8

Year	Club	RUSHING					RECEIVING				
		Att.	Yds.	Avg.	Lg.	TDs	No.	Yds.	Avg.	Lg.	TDs
1978	Houston	302	1,450	4.8	81t	13	12	48	4.0	20	0
1979	Houston	368	1,697	4.6	61t	19	16	94	5.9	46	0
1980	Houston	373	1,934	5.2	55t	13	11	47	4.3	10	0
1981	Houston	361	1,376	3.8	43	10	36	156	4.3	17	0
1982	Houston	157	538	3.4	22	2	18	130	7.2	46	0
1983	Houston	322	1,301	4.0	42	12	19	216	11.4	66	0
1984	Hou.–New Orleans	146	468	3.2	22	4	3	27	9.0	15	0
1985	New Orleans	158	643	4.1	45	1	6	88	14.7	39	0
Totals		**2,187**	**9,407**	**4.3**	**81t**	**74**	**121**	**806**	**6.7**	**66**	**0**

EARNEST BYNER

EARL CAMPBELL

41

CAMPBELL, Scott PITTSBURGH STEELERS
Position: Quarterback; **Birthdate:** 15.04.62
College: Purdue; **Height:** 6–0; **Weight:** 195; **NFL Years:** 2

		PASSING						
Year	Club	Att.	Comp.	Yds.	Lg.	TDs	Int.	Rat.
1984	Pittsburgh	15	8	109	25t	1	1	71.3
1985	Pittsburgh	96	43	612	51	4	6	53.8
Totals		**111**	**51**	**721**	**51**	**5**	**7**	**56.2**

CAPERS, Wayne INDIANAPOLIS COLTS
Position: Wide Receiver; **Birthdate:** 17.05.61
College: Kansas; **Height:** 6–2; **Weight:** 193; **NFL Years:** 3

		RECEIVING				
Year	Club	No.	Yds.	Avg.	Lg.	TDs
1983	Pittsburgh	10	185	18.5	36	1
1984	Pittsburgh	7	81	11.6	19	0
1985	Indianapolis	25	438	17.5	80t	4
Totals		**42**	**704**	**16.8**	**80t**	**5**

CARPENTER, Rob NEW YORK GIANTS
Position: Running Back; **Birthdate:** 20.04.55
College: Miami (Ohio); **Height:** 6–1; **Weight:** 226; **NFL Years:** 9

		RUSHING					RECEIVING				
Year	Club	Att.	Yds.	Avg.	Lg.	TDs	No.	Yds.	Avg.	Lg.	TDs
1977	Houston	144	652	4.5	77t	1	23	156	6.8	27	0
1978	Houston	82	348	4.2	20	5	17	150	8.8	37	0
1979	Houston	92	355	3.9	13	3	16	116	7.3	22	1
1980	Houston	97	359	3.7	46	3	43	346	8.0	25	0
1981	Hou.–N.Y.G.	208	822	4.0	35	5	37	281	7.6	37	1
1982	N.Y. Giants	67	204	3.0	23	1	7	29	4.1	11	0
1983	N.Y. Giants	170	624	3.7	37	4	26	258	9.9	38	2
1984	N.Y. Giants	250	795	3.2	22	7	26	209	8.0	19	1
1985	N.Y. Giants	60	201	3.4	46	0	20	162	8.1	23	0
Totals		**1,170**	**4,360**	**3.7**	**77t**	**29**	**215**	**1,707**	**7.9**	**38**	**5**

CARSON, Carlos KANSAS CITY CHIEFS
Position: Wide Receiver; **Birthdate:** 28.12.58
College: Louisiana State; **Height:** 5—11; **Weight:** 182; **NFL Years:** 6

		RECEIVING				
Year	Club	No.	Yds.	Avg.	Lg.	TDs
1980	Kansas City	5	68	13.6	32	0
1981	Kansas City	7	179	25.6	53t	1
1982	Kansas City	27	494	18.3	51	2
1983	Kansas City	80	1,351	16.9	50t	7
1984	Kansas City	57	1,078	18.9	57	4
1985	Kansas City	47	843	17.9	37t	4
Totals		**223**	**4,013**	**18.0**	**57**	**18**

CARTER, Anthony MINNESOTA VIKINGS
Position: Wide Receiver; **Birthdate:** 17.09.60
College: Michigan; **Height:** 5—11; **Weight:** 162; **NFL Years:** 1

		RECEIVING				
Year	Club	No.	Yds.	Avg.	Lg.	TDs
1985	Minnesota	43	821	19.1	57t	8
Totals		**43**	**821**	**19.1**	**57t**	**8**

CARLOS CARSON

ANTHONY CARTER

43

CARTER, Gerald TAMPA BAY BUCCANEERS
Position: Wide Receiver; **Birthdate:** 19.06.57
College: Texas A&M; **Height:** 6–1; **Weight:** 190; **NFL Years:** 6

		RECEIVING				
Year	Club	No.	Yds.	Avg.	Lg.	TDs
1980	N.Y.J.–T.B.	0	0	0.0	0	0
1981	Tampa Bay	1	10	10.0	10	0
1982	Tampa Bay	10	140	14.0	27	0
1983	Tampa Bay	48	694	14.5	56t	2
1984	Tampa Bay	60	816	13.6	74t	5
1985	Tampa Bay	40	557	13.9	40	3
Totals		**159**	**2,217**	**13.9**	**74t**	**10**

CARTER, Joe MIAMI DOLPHINS
Position: Running Back; **Birthdate:** 23.06.62
College: Alabama; **Height:** 5–11; **Weight:** 198; **NFL Years:** 2

		RUSHING					RECEIVING				
Year	Club	Att.	Yds.	Avg.	Lg.	TDs	No.	Yds.	Avg.	Lg.	TDs
1984	Miami	100	495	5.0	35	1	8	53	6.6	15	0
1985	Miami	14	76	5.4	19	0	2	7	3.5	4	0
Totals		**114**	**571**	**5.0**	**35**	**1**	**10**	**60**	**6.0**	**15**	**0**

GERALD CARTER

JOE CARTER

CARTHON, Maurice NEW YORK GIANTS
Position: Running Back; **Birthdate:** 24.04.61
College: Arkansas State; **Height:** 6–1; **Weight:** 225; **NFL Years:** 1

		RUSHING					**RECEIVING**				
Year	Club	Att.	Yds.	Avg.	Lg.	TDs	No.	Yds.	Avg.	Lg.	TDs
1985	N.Y. Giants	27	70	2.6	12	0	8	81	10.1	22	0
Totals		**27**	**70**	**2.6**	**12**	**0**	**8**	**81**	**10.1**	**22**	**0**

CASTOR, Chris SEATTLE SEAHAWKS
Position: Wide Receiver; **Birthdate:** 13.08.60
College: Duke; **Height:** 6–0; **Weight:** 170; **NFL Years:** 2

		RECEIVING				
Year	Club	No.	Yds.	Avg.	Lg.	TDs
1983	Seattle	0	0	0.0	0	0
1984	Seattle	8	89	11.1	21	0
1985	Seattle			Did not play		
Totals		**8**	**89**	**11.1**	**21**	**0**

CAVANAUGH, Matt PHILADELPHIA EAGLES
Position: Quarterback; **Birthdate:** 27.10.56
College: Pittsburgh; **Height:** 6–2; **Weight:** 202; **NFL Years:** 8

		PASSING						
Year	Club	Att.	Comp.	Yds.	Lg.	TDs	Int.	Rat.
1978	New England	0	0	0	0	0	0	00.0
1979	New England	1	1	10	10	0	0	108.3
1980	New England	105	63	885	40	9	5	95.9
1981	New England	219	115	1,633	65	5	13	60.0
1982	New England	60	27	490	75t	5	5	66.7
1983	San Francisco	0	0	0	0	0	0	00.0
1984	San Francisco	61	33	449	51t	4	0	99.7
1985	San Francisco	54	28	334	41	1	1	69.5
Totals		**500**	**267**	**3,801**	**75t**	**24**	**24**	**74.3**

CHADWICK, Jeff DETROIT LIONS
Position: Wide Receiver; **Birthdate:** 16.12.60
College: Grand Valley State; **Height:** 6–3; **Weight:** 190; **NFL Years:** 3

		RECEIVING				
Year	**Club**	**No.**	**Yds.**	**Avg.**	**Lg.**	**TDs**
1983	Detroit	40	617	15.4	45	4
1984	Detroit	37	540	14.6	46	2
1985	Detroit	25	478	19.1	56	3
Totals		**102**	**1,635**	**16.0**	**56**	**9**

CHANDLER, Wes SAN DIEGO CHARGERS
Position: Wide Receiver; **Birthdate:** 22.08.56
College: Florida; **Height:** 6–0; **Weight:** 182; **NFL Years:** 8

		RECEIVING				
Year	**Club**	**No.**	**Yds.**	**Avg.**	**Lg.**	**TDs**
1978	New Orleans	35	472	13.5	58t	2
1979	New Orleans	65	1,069	16.4	85	6
1980	New Orleans	65	975	15.0	50	6
1981	N.O.–S.D.	69	1,142	16.6	51t	6
1982	San Diego	49	1,032	21.1	66t	9
1983	San Diego	58	845	14.6	44t	5
1984	San Diego	52	708	13.6	63t	6
1985	San Diego	67	1,199	17.9	75t	10
Totals		**460**	**7,442**	**16.2**	**85**	**50**

CHRISTENSEN, Todd LOS ANGELES RAIDERS
Position: Tight End; **Birthdate:** 03.08.56
College: Brigham Young; **Height:** 6–3; **Weight:** 230; **NFL Years:** 7

		RECEIVING				
Year	**Club**	**No.**	**Yds.**	**Avg.**	**Lg.**	**TDs**
1978	Dallas			Did not play		
1979	N.Y.G.–Oak.	0	0	0.0	0	0
1980	Oakland	0	0	0.0	0	0
1981	Oakland	8	115	14.4	30	2
1982	L.A. Raiders	42	510	12.1	50	4

46

WES CHANDLER

DWIGHT CLARK

Year	Club	No.	Yds.	Avg.	Lg.	TDs
1983	L.A. Raiders	92	1,247	13.6	45	12
1984	L.A. Raiders	80	1,007	12.6	38	7
1985	L.A. Raiders	82	987	12.0	48	6
Totals		**304**	**3,866**	**12.7**	**50**	**31**

CLARK, Dwight SAN FRANCISCO 49ers
Position: Wide Receiver; **Birthdate:** 01.08.57
College: Clemson; **Height:** 6–4; **Weight:** 215; **NFL Years:** 7

		RECEIVING				
Year	Club	No.	Yds.	Avg.	Lg.	TDs
1979	San Francisco	18	232	12.9	30	0
1980	San Francisco	82	991	12.1	71t	8
1981	San Francisco	85	1,105	13.0	78t	4
1982	San Francisco	60	913	15.2	51	5
1983	San Francisco	70	840	12.0	46t	8
1984	San Francisco	52	880	16.9	80t	6
1985	San Francisco	54	705	13.1	49t	10
Totals		**421**	**5,666**	**13.5**	**80t**	**41**

CLARK, Gary WASHINGTON REDSKINS
Position: Wide Receiver; **Birthdate:** 01.05.62
College: James Madison; **Height:** 5–9; **Weight:** 173; **NFL Years:** 1

		RECEIVING				
Year	Club	No.	Yds.	Avg.	Lg.	TDs
1985	Washington	72	926	12.9	55	5
Totals		**72**	**926**	**12.9**	**55**	**5**

CLARK, Jessie GREEN BAY PACKERS
Position: Running Back; **Birthdate:** 03.01.60
College: Arkansas; **Height:** 6–0; **Weight:** 233; **NFL Years:** 3

		RUSHING					RECEIVING				
Year	Club	Att.	Yds.	Avg.	Lg.	TDs	No.	Yds.	Avg.	Lg.	TDs
1983	Green Bay	71	328	4.6	42	0	18	279	15.5	75t	1
1984	Green Bay	87	375	4.3	43t	4	29	234	8.1	20	2
1985	Green Bay	147	633	4.3	80	5	24	252	10.5	55t	2
Totals		**305**	**1,336**	**4.4**	**80**	**9**	**71**	**765**	**10.8**	**75t**	**5**

CLAYTON, Mark MIAMI DOLPHINS
Position: Wide Receiver; **Birthdate:** 08.04.61
College: Louisville; **Height:** 5–9; **Weight:** 175; **NFL Years:** 3

		RECEIVING				
Year	Club	No.	Yds.	Avg.	Lg.	TDs
1983	Miami	6	114	19.0	39	1
1984	Miami	73	1,389	19.0	65t	18
1985	Miami	70	996	14.2	45	4
Totals		**149**	**2,499**	**16.8**	**65t**	**23**

COFFMAN, Paul GREEN BAY PACKERS
Position: Tight End; **Birthdate:** 29.03.56
College: Kansas State; **Height:** 6–3; **Weight:** 225; **NFL Years:** 8

		RECEIVING				
Year	Club	No.	Yds.	Avg.	Lg.	TDs
1978	Green Bay	0	0	0.0	0	0

Year	Club	No.	Yds.	Avg.	Lg.	TDs
1979	Green Bay	56	711	12.7	78t	4
1980	Green Bay	42	496	11.8	25	3
1981	Green Bay	55	687	12.5	29	4
1982	Green Bay	23	287	12.5	42	2
1983	Green Bay	54	814	15.1	74	11
1984	Green Bay	43	562	13.1	44t	9
1985	Green Bay	49	666	13.6	32	6
Totals		**322**	**4,223**	**13.1**	**78t**	**39**

COLLINS, Anthony NEW ENGLAND PATRIOTS
Position: Running Back; **Birthdate:** 27.05.59
College: East Carolina; **Height:** 5–11; **Weight:** 212; **NFL Years:** 5

		RUSHING					RECEIVING				
Year	Club	Att.	Yds.	Avg.	Lg.	TDs	No.	Yds.	Avg.	Lg.	TDs
1981	New England	204	873	4.3	29	7	26	232	8.9	22	0
1982	New England	164	632	3.9	54	1	19	187	9.8	33	2
1983	New England	219	1,049	4.8	50t	10	27	257	9.5	20	0
1984	New England	138	550	4.0	21	5	16	100	6.3	19	0
1985	New England	163	657	4.0	28	3	52	549	10.6	49	2
Totals		**888**	**3,761**	**4.2**	**54**	**26**	**140**	**1,325**	**9.5**	**49**	**4**

PAUL COFFMAN

ANTHONY COLLINS

49

COLLINSWORTH, Cris CINCINNATI BENGALS
Position: Wide Receiver; **Birthdate:** 27.01.59
College: Florida; **Height:** 6–5; **Weight:** 192; **NFL Years:** 5

		RECEIVING				
Year	Club	No.	Yds.	Avg.	Lg.	TDs
1981	Cincinnati	67	1,009	15.1	74t	8
1982	Cincinnati	49	700	14.3	50	1
1983	Cincinnati	66	1,130	17.1	63	5
1984	Cincinnati	64	989	15.5	57t	6
1985	Cincinnati	65	1,125	17.3	71	5
Totals		**311**	**4,953**	**15.9**	**74t**	**25**

CRIS COLLINSWORTH

DOUG COSBIE

COOPER, Earl LOS ANGELES RAIDERS
Position: Running Back – Tight End; **Birthdate:** 17.09.57
College: Rice; **Height:** 6–2; **Weight:** 232; **NFL Years:** 6

		RUSHING					RECEIVING				
Year	Club	Att.	Yds.	Avg.	Lg.	TDs	No.	Yds.	Avg.	Lg.	TDs
1980	San Francisco	171	720	4.2	47	5	83	567	6.8	66t	4
1981	San Francisco	98	330	3.4	23	1	51	477	9.4	50	0
1982	San Francisco	24	77	3.2	9	0	19	153	8.1	20	1
1983	San Francisco	0	0	0.0	0	0	15	207	13.8	73t	3
1984	San Francisco	3	13	4.3	7	0	41	459	11.2	26	4
1985	San Francisco	2	12	6.0	14	0	4	45	11.3	20	0
Totals		**298**	**1,152**	**3.9**	**47**	**6**	**213**	**1,908**	**9.0**	**73t**	**12**

CORNWELL, Fred DALLAS COWBOYS
Position: Tight End; **Birthdate:** 07.08.61
College: USC; **Height:** 6–6; **Weight:** 233; **NFL Years:** 2

		RECEIVING				
Year	Club	No.	Yds.	Avg.	Lg.	TDs
1984	Dallas	2	23	11.5	13	1
1985	Dallas	6	77	12.8	32	1
Totals		**8**	**100**	**12.5**	**32**	**2**

COSBIE, Doug DALLAS COWBOYS
Position: Tight End; **Birthdate:** 27.02.56
College: Santa Clara; **Height:** 6–6; **Weight:** 245; **NFL Years:** 7

		RECEIVING				
Year	Club	No.	Yds.	Avg.	Lg.	TDs
1979	Dallas	5	36	7.2	12	0
1980	Dallas	2	11	5.5	6	1
1981	Dallas	17	225	13.2	28	5
1982	Dallas	30	441	14.7	45	4
1983	Dallas	46	588	12.8	61t	6
1984	Dallas	60	789	13.2	36	4
1985	Dallas	64	793	12.4	42	6
Totals		**224**	**2,883**	**12.9**	**61t**	**26**

COX, Arthur ATLANTA FALCONS
Position: Tight End; **Birthdate:** 05.02.61
College: Texas Southern; **Height:** 6–2; **Weight:** 255; **NFL Years:** 3

		RECEIVING				
Year	Club	No.	Yds.	Avg.	Lg.	TDs
1983	Atlanta	9	83	9.2	19	1
1984	Atlanta	34	329	9.7	23t	3
1985	Atlanta	33	454	13.8	62t	2
Totals		**76**	**866**	**11.4**	**62t**	**6**

COX, Steve WASHINGTON REDSKINS
Position: Placekicker; **Birthdate:** 11.05.58
College: Arkansas; **Height:** 6–4; **Weight:** 195; **NFL Years:** 5

		SCORING					
Year	Club	EPA	EPM	FGA	FGM	Lg.	Pts.
1981	Cleveland	0	0	1	0	00	0
1982	Cleveland	0	0	1	0	00	0
1983	Cleveland	0	0	1	1	58	3
1984	Cleveland	0	0	3	1	60	3
1985	Washington	0	0	1	0	00	0
Totals		**0**	**0**	**7**	**2**	**60**	**6**

CRAIG, Roger SAN FRANCISCO 49ers
Position: Running Back; **Birthdate:** 10.07.60
College: Nebraska; **Height:** 6–0; **Weight:** 222; **NFL Years:** 3

		RUSHING					RECEIVING				
Year	Club	Att.	Yds.	Avg.	Lg.	TDs	No.	Yds.	Avg.	Lg.	TDs
1983	San Francisco	176	725	4.1	71	8	48	427	8.9	23	4
1984	San Francisco	155	649	4.2	28	7	71	675	9.5	64t	3
1985	San Francisco	214	1,050	4.9	62t	9	92	1,016	11.0	73	6
Totals		**545**	**2,424**	**4.4**	**71**	**24**	**211**	**2,118**	**10.0**	**73**	**13**

CRIBBS, Joe BUFFALO BILLS
Position: Running Back; **Birthdate:** 05.01.58
College: Auburn; **Height:** 5–11; **Weight:** 193; **NFL Years:** 5

		RUSHING					RECEIVING				
Year	Club	Att.	Yds.	Avg.	Lg.	TDs	No.	Yds.	Avg.	Lg.	TDs
1980	Buffalo	306	1,185	3.9	48	11	52	415	8.0	21t	1
1981	Buffalo	257	1,097	4.3	35	3	40	603	15.1	65t	7
1982	Buffalo	134	633	4.7	62t	3	13	99	7.6	31	0
1983	Buffalo	263	1,131	4.3	45	3	57	524	9.2	33t	7
1984						Did not play					
1985	Buffalo	122	399	3.3	16	1	18	142	7.9	23	0
Totals		**1,082**	**4,445**	**4.1**	**62t**	**21**	**180**	**1,783**	**9.9**	**65t**	**15**

ARTHUR COX

ROGER CRAIG

CRUTCHFIELD, Dwayne HOUSTON OILERS
Position: Running Back; **Birthdate:** 30.09.59
College: Iowa State; **Height:** 6–0; **Weight:** 240; **NFL Years:** 3

		RUSHING					RECEIVING				
Year	Club	Att.	Yds.	Avg.	Lg.	TDs	No.	Yds.	Avg.	Lg.	TDs
1982	N.Y. Jets	22	78	3.5	8	1	0	0	0.0	0	0
1983	N.Y.J.–Hou.	140	578	4.1	17	3	19	133	7.0	15	0
1984	L.A. Rams	73	337	4.6	36	1	2	11	5.5	7	1
1985	Houston					Did not play					
Totals		**235**	**993**	**4.2**	**36**	**5**	**21**	**144**	**6.9**	**15**	**1**

CUNNINGHAM, Bennie PITTSBURGH STEELERS
Position: Tight End; **Birthdate:** 23.12.54
College: Clemson; **Height:** 6–5; **Weight:** 265; **NFL Years:** 10

		RECEIVING			
Year	Club	No.	Yds.	Avg.	Lg.	TDs
1976	Pittsburgh	5	49	9.8	20	1
1977	Pittsburgh	20	347	17.4	43t	2
1978	Pittsburgh	16	321	20.1	48	2
1979	Pittsburgh	36	512	14.2	28t	4
1980	Pittsburgh	18	232	12.9	35	2
1981	Pittsburgh	41	574	14.0	30	3
1982	Pittsburgh	21	277	13.2	31	2
1983	Pittsburgh	35	442	12.6	29	3
1984	Pittsburgh	4	64	16.0	29	1
1985	Pittsburgh	6	61	10.2	17	0
Totals		**202**	**2,879**	**14.3**	**48**	**20**

CUNNINGHAM, Randall PHILADELPHIA EAGLES
Position: Quarterback; **Birthdate:** 27.03.63
College: Nevada-Las Vegas; **Height:** 6–4; **Weight:** 192; **NFL Years:** 1

		PASSING						
Year	Club	Att.	Comp.	Yds.	Lg.	TDs	Int.	Rat.
1985	Philadelphia	81	34	548	69	1	8	29.8
Totals		**81**	**34**	**548**	**69**	**1**	**8**	**29.8**

D'ADDIO, Dave DETROIT LIONS
Position: Running Back; **Birthdate:** 13.07.61
College: Maryland; **Height:** 6–1; **Weight:** 229; **NFL Years:** 1

Year	Club	RUSHING					RECEIVING				
		Att.	Yds.	Avg.	Lg.	TDs	No.	Yds.	Avg.	Lg.	TDs
1984	Detroit	7	46	6.6	14	0	1	12	12.0	12	0
1985	Detroit					Did not play					
Totals		**7**	**46**	**6.6**	**14**	**0**	**1**	**12**	**12.0**	**12**	**0**

BENNIE CUNNINGHAM

DAVE D'ADDIO

DANIELSON, Gary CLEVELAND BROWNS
Position: Quarterback; **Birthdate:** 10.09.51
College: Purdue; **Height:** 6–2; **Weight:** 196; **NFL Years:** 9

		PASSING						
Year	Club	Att.	Comp.	Yds.	Lg.	TDs	Int.	Rat.
1976	Detroit	0	0	0	0	0	0	00.0
1977	Detroit	100	42	445	61	1	5	38.1
1978	Detroit	351	199	2,294	47	18	17	73.6
1979	Detroit			Did not play				
1980	Detroit	417	244	3,223	87t	13	11	82.6
1981	Detroit	96	56	784	45	3	5	73.4
1982	Detroit	197	100	1,343	70t	10	14	60.3
1983	Detroit	113	59	720	54	7	4	78.0
1984	Detroit	410	252	3,076	77t	17	15	83.1
1985	Cleveland	163	97	1,274	72t	8	6	85.3
Totals		**1,847**	**1,049**	**13,159**	**87t**	**77**	**77**	**75.6**

GARY DANIELSON

RON DAVENPORT

DAVENPORT, Ron MIAMI DOLPHINS
Position: Running Back; **Birthdate:** 22.12.62
College: Louisville; **Height:** 6–2; **Weight:** 230; **NFL Years:** 1

		RUSHING					RECEIVING				
Year	Club	Att.	Yds.	Avg.	Lg.	TDs	No.	Yds.	Avg.	Lg.	TDs
1985	Miami	98	370	3.8	33	11	13	74	5.7	17t	2
Totals		**98**	**370**	**3.8**	**33**	**11**	**13**	**74**	**5.7**	**17t**	**2**

DAVIS, Johnny CLEVELAND BROWNS
Position: Running Back; **Birthdate:** 17.07.56
College: Alabama; **Height:** 6–1; **Weight:** 235; **NFL Years:** 8

		RUSHING					RECEIVING				
Year	Club	Att.	Yds.	Avg.	Lg.	TDs	No.	Yds.	Avg.	Lg.	TDs
1978	Tampa Bay	97	370	3.8	18	3	5	13	2.6	7	0
1979	Tampa Bay	59	221	3.7	18	2	5	57	11.4	24	0
1980	Tampa Bay	39	130	3.3	8	1	4	17	4.3	9	0
1981	San Francisco	94	297	3.2	14	7	3	−1	−0.3	3	0
1982	Cleveland	4	3	0.8	2	1	0	0	0.0	0	0
1983	Cleveland	13	42	3.2	16	0	5	20	4.0	10	0
1984	Cleveland	3	15	5.0	8	1	0	0	0.0	0	0
1985	Cleveland	4	9	2.3	5	0	0	0	0.0	0	0
Totals		**313**	**1,087**	**3.5**	**18**	**15**	**22**	**106**	**4.8**	**24**	**0**

DAWSON, Lin NEW ENGLAND PATRIOTS
Position: Tight End; **Birthdate:** 24.06.59
College: North Carolina State; **Height:** 6–3; **Weight:** 240; **NFL Years:** 5

		RECEIVING				
Year	Club	No.	Yds.	Avg.	Lg.	TDs
1981	New England	7	126	18.0	42	0
1982	New England	13	160	12.3	26	1
1983	New England	9	84	9.3	14	1
1984	New England	39	427	10.9	27	4
1985	New England	17	148	8.7	26	0
Totals		**85**	**945**	**11.1**	**42**	**6**

DeBERG, Steve TAMPA BAY BUCCANEERS
Position: Quarterback; **Birthdate:** 19.01.54
College: San Jose State; **Height:** 6–3; **Weight:** 205; **NFL Years:** 9

				PASSING				
Year	**Club**	**Att.**	**Comp.**	**Yds.**	**Lg.**	**TDs**	**Int.**	**Rat.**
1977	San Francisco	0	0	0	0	0	0	00.0
1978	San Francisco	302	137	1,570	58t	8	22	39.8
1979	San Francisco	578	347	3,652	50	17	21	73.1
1980	San Francisco	321	186	1,998	93t	12	17	66.5
1981	Denver	108	64	797	44	6	6	77.6
1982	Denver	223	131	1,405	51t	7	11	67.2
1983	Denver	215	119	1,617	54	9	7	79.9
1984	Tampa Bay	509	308	3,554	55	19	18	79.3
1985	Tampa Bay	370	197	2,488	57	19	18	71.3
Totals		**2,626**	**1,489**	**17,081**	**93t**	**97**	**120**	**69.7**

STEVE DEBERG

AL DEL GRECO

DEL GRECO, Al GREEN BAY PACKERS
Position: Placekicker; **Birthdate:** 02.03.62
College: Auburn; **Height:** 5–10; **Weight:** 195; **NFL Years:** 2

		SCORING					
Year	Club	EPA	EPM	FGA	FGM	Lg.	Pts.
1984	Green Bay	34	34	12	9	45	61
1985	Green Bay	40	38	26	19	46	95
Totals		**74**	**72**	**38**	**28**	**46**	**156**

DENNARD, Preston GREEN BAY PACKERS
Position: Wide Receiver; **Birthdate:** 28.11.55
College: New Mexico; **Height:** 6–1; **Weight:** 183; **NFL Years:** 8

		RECEIVING				
Year	Club	No.	Yds.	Avg.	Lg.	TDs
1978	L.A. Rams	3	35	11.7	15	0
1979	L.A. Rams	43	766	17.8	50	4
1980	L.A. Rams	36	596	16.6	44	6
1981	L.A. Rams	49	821	16.8	64	4
1982	L.A. Rams	25	383	15.3	39	2
1983	L.A. Rams	33	465	14.1	61t	5
1984	Buffalo	30	417	13.9	68t	7
1985	Green Bay	13	182	14.0	34	2
Totals		**232**	**3,665**	**15.8**	**68t**	**30**

DENNISON, Glenn NEW YORK JETS
Position: Tight End; **Birthdate:** 17.11.61
College: Miami; **Height:** 6–3; **Weight:** 225; **NFL Years:** 1

		RECEIVING				
Year	Club	No.	Yds.	Avg.	Lg.	TDs
1984	N.Y. Jets	16	141	8.8	20	1
1985	N.Y. Jets			Did not play		
Totals		**16**	**141**	**8.8**	**20**	**1**

ERIC DICKERSON

LYNN DICKEY

DICKERSON, Eric LOS ANGELES RAMS
Position: Running Back; **Birthdate:** 02.09.60
College: SMU; **Height:** 6–3; **Weight:** 220; **NFL Years:** 3

Year	Club		RUSHING					RECEIVING			
		Att.	Yds.	Avg.	Lg.	TDs	No.	Yds.	Avg.	Lg.	TDs
1983	L.A. Rams	390	1,808	4.6	85t	18	51	404	7.9	37t	2
1984	L.A. Rams	379	2,105	5.6	66	14	21	139	6.6	19	0
1985	L.A. Rams	292	1,234	4.2	43	12	20	126	6.3	33	0
Totals		**1,061**	**5,147**	**4.9**	**85t**	**44**	**92**	**669**	**7.3**	**37t**	**2**

DICKEY, Curtis CLEVELAND BROWNS
Position: Running Back; **Birthdate:** 27.11.56
College: Texas A&M; **Height:** 6–1; **Weight:** 220; **NFL Years:** 6

Year	Club		RUSHING					RECEIVING			
		Att.	Yds.	Avg.	Lg.	TDs	No.	Yds.	Avg.	Lg.	TDs
1980	Baltimore	176	800	4.5	51t	11	25	204	8.2	32	2
1981	Baltimore	164	779	4.8	67t	7	37	419	11.3	50	3
1982	Baltimore	66	232	3.5	25	1	21	228	10.9	34	0
1983	Baltimore	254	1,122	4.4	56	4	24	483	20.1	72t	3

Year	Club	Att.	Yds.	Avg.	Lg.	TDs	No.	Yds.	Avg.	Lg.	TDs
1984	Indianapolis	131	523	4.0	30	3	14	135	9.6	33	0
1985	Ind.-Clev.	11	40	3.6	11	0	3	30	10.0	11	0
Totals		802	3,496	4.4	67t	26	124	1,499	12.1	72t	8

DICKEY, Lynn
Position: Quarterback; **Birthdate:** 19.10.49
College: Kansas State; **Height:** 6–4; **Weight:** 203; **NFL Years:** 13

				PASSING				
Year	Club	Att.	Comp.	Yds.	Lg.	TDs	Int.	Rat.
1971	Houston	57	19	315	42	0	9	13.3
1972	Houston			Did not play				
1973	Houston	120	71	888	66t	6	10	64.3
1974	Houston	113	63	704	59	2	8	51.0
1975	Houston	4	2	46	28	0	1	52.1
1976	Green Bay	243	115	1,465	69t	7	14	52.1
1977	Green Bay	220	113	1,346	95t	5	14	51.4
1978	Green Bay			Did not play				
1979	Green Bay	119	60	787	52t	5	4	71.5
1980	Green Bay	478	278	3,529	69t	15	25	70.0
1981	Green Bay	354	204	2,593	75t	17	15	79.1
1982	Green Bay	218	124	1,790	80t	12	14	75.4
1983	Green Bay	484	289	4,458	75t	32	29	87.3
1984	Green Bay	401	237	3,195	79t	25	19	85.6
1985	Green Bay	314	172	2,206	63	15	17	70.4
Totals		3,125	1,747	23,322	95t	141	179	70.9

DIDIER, Clint WASHINGTON REDSKINS
Position: Tight End; **Birthdate:** 04.04.59
College: Portland State; **Height:** 6–5; **Weight:** 240; **NFL Years:** 4

				RECEIVING		
Year	Club	No.	Yds.	Avg.	Lg.	TDs
1981	Washington			Did not play		
1982	Washington	2	10	5.0	8	1
1983	Washington	9	153	17.0	40t	4
1984	Washington	30	350	11.7	44	5
1985	Washington	41	433	10.6	29	4
Totals		82	946	11.5	44	14

DILS, Steve LOS ANGELES RAMS
Position: Quarterback; **Birthdate:** 08.12.55
College: Stanford; **Height:** 6–1; **Weight:** 191; **NFL Years:** 7

		PASSING						
Year	Club	Att.	Comp.	Yds.	Lg.	TDs	Int.	Rat.
1979	Minnesota	0	0	0	0	0	0	00.0
1980	Minnesota	51	32	352	58t	3	0	102.8
1981	Minnesota	102	54	607	44	1	2	66.0
1982	Minnesota	26	11	68	12	0	0	49.8
1983	Minnesota	444	239	2,840	68	11	16	66.8
1984	Minn.-L.A. Rams	7	4	44	14t	1	1	75.9
1985	L.A. Rams	0	0	0	0	0	0	00.0
Totals		**630**	**240**	**3,911**	**68**	**16**	**19**	**68.8**

DOORNINK, Dan SEATTLE SEAHAWKS
Position: Running Back; **Birthdate:** 01.02.56
College: Washington State; **Height:** 6–3; **Weight:** 210; **NFL Years:** 8

		RUSHING					RECEIVING				
Year	Club	Att.	Yds.	Avg.	Lg.	TDs	No.	Yds.	Avg.	Lg.	TDs
1978	N.Y. Giants	60	306	5.1	24	1	12	66	5.5	24	0
1979	Seattle	152	500	3.3	26t	8	54	432	8.0	41	1
1980	Seattle	100	344	3.4	22	3	31	237	7.6	16	2
1981	Seattle	65	194	3.0	11	1	27	350	13.0	80t	4
1982	Seattle	45	178	4.0	46	0	22	176	8.0	44	0
1983	Seattle	40	99	2.5	9	2	24	328	13.7	47	2
1984	Seattle	57	215	3.8	25	0	31	365	11.8	32	2
1985	Seattle	4	0	0.0	3	0	8	52	6.5	19	0
Totals		**523**	**1,836**	**3.5**	**46**	**15**	**209**	**2,006**	**9.6**	**80t**	**11**

DORSETT, Tony DALLAS COWBOYS
Position: Running Back; **Birthdate:** 07.04.54
College: Pittsburgh; **Height:** 5–11; **Weight:** 185; **NFL Years:** 9

		RUSHING					RECEIVING				
Year	Club	Att.	Yds.	Avg.	Lg.	TDs	No.	Yds.	Avg.	Lg.	TDs
1977	Dallas	208	1,007	4.8	84t	12	29	273	9.4	23	1
1978	Dallas	290	1,325	4.6	63	7	37	378	10.2	91t	2

TONY DORSETT

CHRIS DRESSEL

Year	Club	Att.	Yds.	Avg.	Lg.	TDs	No.	Yds.	Avg.	Lg.	TDs
1979	Dallas	250	1,107	4.4	41	6	45	375	8.3	32	1
1980	Dallas	278	1,185	4.3	56	11	34	263	7.7	27	0
1981	Dallas	342	1,646	4.8	75t	4	32	325	10.2	73t	2
1982	Dallas	177	745	4.2	99t	5	24	179	7.5	18	0
1983	Dallas	289	1,321	4.6	77	8	40	287	7.2	24	1
1984	Dallas	302	1,189	3.9	31t	6	51	459	9.0	68t	1
1985	Dallas	305	1,307	4.3	60t	7	46	449	9.8	56t	3
Totals		**2,441**	**10,832**	**4.4**	**99t**	**66**	**338**	**2,988**	**8.8**	**91t**	**11**

DRESSEL, Chris HOUSTON OILERS
Position: Tight End; **Birthdate:** 07.02.61
College: Stanford; **Height:** 6–4; **Weight:** 238; **NFL Years:** 3

			RECEIVING			
Year	Club	No.	Yds.	Avg.	Lg.	TDs
1983	Houston	32	316	9.9	35t	4
1984	Houston	40	378	9.5	42	2
1985	Houston	3	17	5.7	12	1
Totals		**75**	**711**	**9.5**	**42**	**7**

DUCKETT, Kenny DALLAS COWBOYS
Position: Wide Receiver; **Birthdate:** 01.10.59
College: Wake Forest; **Height:** 5–11; **Weight:** 183; **NFL Years:** 4

		RECEIVING				
Year	**Club**	**No.**	**Yds.**	**Avg.**	**Lg.**	**TDs**
1982	New Orleans	12	196	16.3	31	2
1983	New Orleans	19	283	14.9	48	2
1984	New Orleans	3	24	8.0	11	0
1985	N.O.–Dallas	0	0	0.0	0	0
Totals		**34**	**503**	**14.8**	**48**	**4**

DUCKWORTH, Bobby LOS ANGELES RAMS
Position: Wide Receiver; **Birthdate:** 27.11.58
College: Arkansas; **Height:** 6–3; **Weight:** 196; **NFL Years:** 4

		RECEIVING				
Year	**Club**	**No.**	**Yds.**	**Avg.**	**Lg.**	**TDs**
1981	San Diego			Did not play		
1982	San Diego	2	77	38.5	55	0
1983	San Diego	20	422	21.1	59t	5
1984	San Diego	25	715	28.6	88t	4
1985	L.A. Rams	25	422	16.9	42	3
Totals		**72**	**1,636**	**22.7**	**88t**	**12**

DUNCAN, Clyde ST. LOUIS CARDINALS
Position: Wide Receiver; **Birthdate:** 05.02.61
College: Tennessee; **Height:** 6–2; **Weight:** 211; **NFL Years:** 2

		RECEIVING				
Year	**Club**	**No.**	**Yds.**	**Avg.**	**Lg.**	**TDs**
1984	St. Louis	0	0	0.0	0	0
1985	St. Louis	4	39	9.8	14	1
Totals		**4**	**39**	**9.8**	**14**	**1**

DUNSMORE, Pat CHICAGO BEARS
Position: Tight End; **Birthdate:** 02.10.59
College: Drake; **Height:** 6–3; **Weight:** 237; **NFL Years:** 2

		RECEIVING				
Year	Club	No.	Yds.	Avg.	Lg.	TDs
1983	Chicago	8	102	12.8	24	0
1984	Chicago	9	106	11.8	25	1
1985	Chicago			Did not play		
Totals		**17**	**208**	**12.2**	**25**	**1**

DUPER, Mark MIAMI DOLPHINS
Position: Wide Receiver; **Birthdate:** 25.01.59
College: Northwestern State La; **Height:** 5–9; **Weight:** 187; **NFL Years:** 4

		RECEIVING				
Year	Club	No.	Yds.	Avg.	Lg.	TDs
1982	Miami	0	0	0.0	0	0
1983	Miami	51	1,003	19.7	85t	10
1984	Miami	71	1,306	18.4	80t	8
1985	Miami	35	650	18.6	67t	3
Totals		**157**	**2,959**	**18.8**	**85t**	**21**

BOBBY DUCKWORTH

MARK DUPER

EASON, Tony NEW ENGLAND PATRIOTS
Position: Quarterback; **Birthdate:** 08.10.59
College: Illinois; **Height:** 6–4; **Weight:** 212; **NFL Years:** 3

		PASSING						
Year	Club	Att.	Comp.	Yds.	Lg.	TDs	Int.	Rat.
1983	New England	95	46	557	35	1	5	48.4
1984	New England	431	259	3,228	76t	23	8	93.4
1985	New England	299	168	2,156	90t	11	17	67.5
Totals		**825**	**473**	**5,941**	**90t**	**35**	**30**	**78.9**

EDWARDS, Stan HOUSTON OILERS
Position: Running Back; **Birthdate:** 20.05.60
College: Michigan; **Height:** 6–0; **Weight:** 210; **NFL Years:** 4

		RUSHING					RECEIVING				
Year	Club	Att.	Yds.	Avg.	Lg.	TDs	No.	Yds.	Avg.	Lg.	TDs
1982	Houston	15	58	3.9	8	0	9	53	5.9	21	0
1983	Houston	16	40	2.5	9	0	9	79	8.8	20	1
1984	Houston	60	267	4.5	20	1	20	151	7.6	20	0
1985	Houston	25	96	3.8	19	1	7	71	10.1	31	0
Totals		**116**	**461**	**4.0**	**20**	**2**	**45**	**354**	**7.9**	**31**	**1**

TONY EASON

HENRY ELLARD

ELLARD, Henry LOS ANGELES RAMS
Position: Wide Receiver; **Birthdate:** 21.07.61
College: Fresno State; **Height:** 5–11; **Weight:** 170; **NFL Years:** 3

		RECEIVING				
Year	Club	No.	Yds.	Avg.	Lg.	TDs
1983	L.A. Rams	16	268	16.8	44	0
1984	L.A. Rams	34	622	18.3	63t	6
1985	L.A. Rams	54	811	15.0	64t	5
Totals		**104**	**1,701**	**16.4**	**64t**	**11**

ELLERSON, Gary GREEN BAY PACKERS
Position: Running Back; **Birthdate:** 17.07.63
College: Wisconsin; **Height:** 5–11; **Weight:** 220; **NFL Years:** 1

		RUSHING					**RECEIVING**				
Year	Club	Att.	Yds.	Avg.	Lg.	TDs	No.	Yds.	Avg.	Lg.	TDs
1985	Green Bay	32	205	6.4	37t	2	2	15	7.5	11	0
Totals		**32**	**205**	**6.4**	**37t**	**2**	**2**	**15**	**7.5**	**11**	**0**

ELLIS, Gerry GREEN BAY PACKERS
Position: Running Back; **Birthdate:** 12.11.57
College: Missouri; **Height:** 5–11; **Weight:** 225; **NFL Years:** 6

		RUSHING					**RECEIVING**				
Year	Club	Att.	Yds.	Avg.	Lg.	TDs	No.	Yds.	Avg.	Lg.	TDs
1980	Green Bay	126	545	4.3	22	5	48	496	10.3	69t	3
1981	Green Bay	196	860	4.4	29	4	65	499	7.7	46t	3
1982	Green Bay	62	228	3.7	29	1	18	140	7.8	20	0
1983	Green Bay	141	696	4.9	71	4	52	603	11.6	56	2
1984	Green Bay	123	581	4.7	50	4	36	312	8.7	22	2
1985	Green Bay	104	571	5.5	39t	5	24	206	8.6	35	0
Totals		**752**	**3,481**	**4.6**	**71**	**23**	**243**	**2,256**	**9.3**	**69t**	**10**

ELWAY, John DENVER BRONCOS
Position: Quarterback; **Birthdate:** 28.06.60
College: Stanford; **Height:** 6–3; **Weight:** 210; **NFL Years:** 3

		PASSING						
Year	Club	Att.	Comp.	Yds.	Lg.	TDs	Int.	Rat.
1983	Denver	259	123	1,663	49t	7	14	54.9
1984	Denver	380	214	2,598	73	18	15	76.8
1985	Denver	605	327	3,891	65t	22	23	70.2
Totals		**1,244**	**664**	**8,152**	**73**	**47**	**52**	**69.0**

EPPS, Phil GREEN BAY PACKERS
Position: Wide Receiver; **Birthdate:** 11.11.59
College: Texas Christian; **Height:** 5–10; **Weight:** 165; **NFL Years:** 4

		RECEIVING			
Year	Club	No.	Yds.	Avg.	Lg.	TDs
1982	Green Bay	10	226	22.6	50	2
1983	Green Bay	18	313	17.4	45	0
1984	Green Bay	26	435	16.7	56	3
1985	Green Bay	44	683	15.5	63	3
Totals		**98**	**1,657**	**16.9**	**63**	**8**

ERENBERG, Rich PITTSBURGH STEELERS
Position: Running Back; **Birthdate:** 17.04.62
College: Colgate; **Height:** 5–10; **Weight:** 200; **NFL Years:** 2

		RUSHING					RECEIVING				
Year	Club	Att.	Yds.	Avg.	Lg.	TDs	No.	Yds.	Avg.	Lg.	TDs
1984	Pittsburgh	115	405	3.5	31t	2	38	358	9.4	25	1
1985	Pittsburgh	17	67	3.9	12	0	33	326	9.9	35	3
Totals		**132**	**472**	**3.6**	**31t**	**2**	**71**	**684**	**9.6**	**35**	**4**

ESIASON, Boomer CINCINNATI BENGALS
Position: Quarterback; **Birthdate:** 17.04.61
College: Maryland; **Height:** 6–4; **Weight:** 220; **NFL Years:** 2

| | | PASSING | | | | | | |
Year	Club	Att.	Comp.	Yds.	Lg.	TDs	Int.	Rat.
1984	Cincinnati	102	51	530	36	3	3	62.9
1985	Cincinnati	431	251	3,443	68t	27	12	93.2
Totals		**533**	**302**	**3,973**	**68t**	**30**	**15**	**87.4**

EVERETT, Major PHILADELPHIA EAGLES
Position: Running Back; **Birthdate:** 04.01.60
College: Mississippi College; **Height:** 5–11; **Weight:** 218; **NFL Years:** 3

| | | RUSHING | | | | | RECEIVING | | | | |
Year	Club	Att.	Yds.	Avg.	Lg.	TDs	No.	Yds.	Avg.	Lg.	TDs
1983	Philadelphia	5	7	1.4	7	0	2	18	9.0	11	0
1984	Philadelphia	0	0	0.0	0	0	0	0	0.0	0	0
1985	Philadelphia	4	13	3.3	8	0	4	25	6.3	11	0
Totals		**9**	**20**	**2.2**	**8**	**0**	**6**	**43**	**7.2**	**11**	**0**

JOHN ELWAY

PHIL EPPS

JOE FERGUSON

EARL FERRELL

FERGUSON, Joe DETROIT LIONS
Position: Quarterback; **Birthdate:** 23.04.50
College: Arkansas; **Height:** 6–1; **Weight:** 195; **NFL Years:** 13

				PASSING				
Year	Club	Att.	Comp.	Yds.	Lg.	TDs	Int.	Rat.
1973	Buffalo	164	73	939	42	4	10	45.6
1974	Buffalo	232	119	1,588	55t	12	12	69.0
1975	Buffalo	321	169	2,426	77t	25	17	81.3
1976	Buffalo	151	74	1,086	58t	9	1	90.0
1977	Buffalo	457	221	2,803	42	12	24	54.6
1978	Buffalo	330	175	2,136	92t	16	15	70.5
1979	Buffalo	458	238	3,572	84t	14	15	74.5
1980	Buffalo	439	251	2,805	69	20	18	74.6
1981	Buffalo	498	252	3,652	67t	24	20	74.1
1982	Buffalo	264	144	1,597	47	7	16	56.3

Year	Club	Att.	Comp.	Yds.	Lg.	TDs	Int.	Rat.
1983	Buffalo	508	281	2,995	43t	26	25	69.3
1984	Buffalo	344	191	1,991	68t	12	17	63.5
1985	Detroit	54	31	364	38	2	3	67.2
Totals		**4,220**	**2,219**	**27,954**	**92t**	**183**	**193**	**68.9**

FERRAGAMO, Vince GREEN BAY PACKERS
Position: Quarterback; **Birthdate:** 24.04.54
College: Nebraska; **Height:** 6–3; **Weight:** 212; **NFL Years:** 8

				PASSING				
Year	Club	Att.	Comp.	Yds.	Lg.	TDs	Int.	Rat.
1977	L.A. Rams	15	9	83	17t	2	0	114.7
1978	L.A. Rams	20	7	114	28	0	2	15.4
1979	L.A. Rams	110	53	778	71t	5	10	48.8
1980	L.A. Rams	404	240	3,199	74t	30	19	89.7
1981				Did not play				
1982	L.A. Rams	209	118	1,609	85t	9	9	77.7
1983	L.A. Rams	464	274	3,276	61t	22	23	75.9
1984	L.A. Rams	66	29	317	68	2	8	29.2
1985	Buff.-Green Bay	287	149	1,677	48	5	17	50.8
Totals		**1,575**	**879**	**11,053**	**85t**	**75**	**88**	**70.4**

FERRELL, Earl ST. LOUIS CARDINALS
Position: Running Back; **Birthdate:** 27.03.58
College: East Tennessee State; **Height:** 6–0; **Weight:** 224; **NFL Years:** 4

		RUSHING					RECEIVING				
Year	Club	Att.	Yds.	Avg.	Lg.	TDs	No.	Yds.	Avg.	Lg.	TDs
1982	St. Louis	0	0	0.0	0	0	0	0	0.0	0	0
1983	St. Louis	7	53	7.6	21	1	0	0	0.0	0	0
1984	St. Louis	44	203	4.6	25	1	26	218	8.4	21	1
1985	St. Louis	46	208	4.5	30	2	25	277	11.1	30	2
Totals		**97**	**464**	**4.8**	**30**	**4**	**51**	**495**	**9.7**	**30**	**3**

FOUTS, Dan SAN DIEGO CHARGERS
Position: Quarterback; **Birthdate:** 10.06.51
College: Oregon; **Height:** 6–3; **Weight:** 205; **NFL Years:** 13

		PASSING						
Year	Club	Att.	Comp.	Yds.	Lg.	TDs	Int.	Rat.
1973	San Diego	194	87	1,126	69t	6	13	46.0
1974	San Diego	237	115	1,732	75t	8	13	61.4
1975	San Diego	195	106	1,396	57	2	10	59.3
1976	San Diego	359	208	2,535	81t	14	15	75.3
1977	San Diego	109	69	869	67t	4	6	77.5
1978	San Diego	381	224	2,999	55t	24	20	83.2
1979	San Diego	530	332	4,082	65t	24	24	82.6
1980	San Diego	589	348	4,715	65	30	24	84.6
1981	San Diego	609	360	4,802	67t	33	17	90.6
1982	San Diego	330	204	2,883	44t	17	11	93.6
1983	San Diego	340	215	2,975	59t	20	15	92.5
1984	San Diego	507	317	3,740	61t	19	17	83.4
1985	San Diego	430	254	3,638	75t	27	20	88.1
Totals		**4,810**	**2,839**	**37,492**	**81t**	**228**	**205**	**81.8**

FOWLER, Todd DALLAS COWBOYS
Position: Running Back; **Birthdate:** 09.06.62
College: Stephen F. Austin; **Height:** 6–3; **Weight:** 218; **NFL Years:** 1

		RUSHING					RECEIVING				
Year	Club	Att.	Yds.	Avg.	Lg.	TDs	No.	Yds.	Avg.	Lg.	TDs
1985	Dallas	7	25	3.6	6	0	5	24	4.8	10	0
Totals		**7**	**25**	**3.6**	**6**	**0**	**5**	**24**	**4.8**	**10**	**0**

FRANCIS, Russ SAN FRANCISCO 49ers
Position: Tight End; **Birthdate:** 03.04.53
College: Oregon; **Height:** 6–6; **Weight:** 242; **NFL Years:** 10

		RECEIVING				
Year	Club	No.	Yds.	Avg.	Lg.	TDs
1975	New England	35	636	18.2	48	4
1976	New England	26	367	14.1	38t	3
1977	New England	16	229	14.3	31t	4

Year	Club	No.	Yds.	Avg.	Lg.	TDs
1978	New England	39	543	13.9	53	4
1979	New England	39	557	14.3	44	5
1980	New England	41	664	16.2	39t	8
1981	New England			Did not play		
1982	San Francisco	23	278	12.1	26	2
1983	San Francisco	33	357	10.8	25	4
1984	San Francisco	23	285	12.4	32	2
1985	San Francisco	44	478	10.9	25	3
Totals		**319**	**4,394**	**13.8**	**53**	**39**

FRANK, John SAN FRANCISCO 49ers
Position: Tight End; **Birthdate:** 17.04.62
College: Ohio State; **Height:** 6–3; **Weight:** 225; **NFL Years:** 2

		RECEIVING				
Year	Club	No.	Yds.	Avg.	Lg.	TDs
1984	San Francisco	7	60	8.6	21	1
1985	San Francisco	7	50	7.1	14	1
Totals		**14**	**110**	**7.9**	**21**	**2**

RUSS FRANCIS

JOHN FRANK

FRANKLIN, Byron SEATTLE SEAHAWKS
Position: Wide Receiver; **Birthdate:** 04.09.58
College: Auburn; **Height:** 6–1; **Weight:** 181; **NFL Years:** 4

		RECEIVING				
Year	Club	No.	Yds.	Avg.	Lg.	TDs
1981	Buffalo	2	29	14.5	16	0
1982	Buffalo			Did not play		
1983	Buffalo	30	452	15.1	43t	4
1984	Buffalo	69	862	12.5	64t	4
1985	Seattle	10	119	11.9	28	0
Totals		**111**	**1,462**	**13.2**	**64t**	**8**

FRANKLIN, Tony NEW ENGLAND PATRIOTS
Position: Placekicker; **Birthdate:** 18.11.56
College: Texas A&M; **Height:** 5–8; **Weight:** 182; **NFL Years:** 7

		SCORING					
Year	Club	EPA	EPM	FGA	FGM	Lg.	Pts.
1979	Philadelphia	39	36	31	23	59	105
1980	Philadelphia	48	48	31	16	51	96
1981	Philadelphia	43	41	31	20	50	101
1982	Philadelphia	25	23	9	6	47	41
1983	Philadelphia	27	24	26	15	52	69
1984	New England	42	42	28	22	48	108
1985	New England	41	40	30	24	50	112
Totals		**265**	**254**	**186**	**126**	**59**	**632**

FRYAR, Irving NEW ENGLAND PATRIOTS
Position: Wide Receiver; **Birthdate:** 28.09.62
College: Nebraska; **Height:** 6–0; **Weight:** 200; **NFL Years:** 2

		RECEIVING				
Year	Club	No.	Yds.	Avg.	Lg.	TDs
1984	New England	11	164	14.9	26	1
1985	New England	39	670	17.2	56	7
Totals		**50**	**834**	**16.7**	**56**	**8**

TONY FRANKLIN

IRVING FRYAR

FULLER, Steve CHICAGO BEARS
Position: Quarterback; **Birthdate:** 05.01.57
College: Clemson; **Height:** 6–4; **Weight:** 195; **NFL Years:** 7

				PASSING				
Year	Club	Att.	Comp.	Yds.	Lg.	TDs	Int.	Rat.
1979	Kansas City	270	146	1,484	40	6	14	55.8
1980	Kansas City	320	193	2,250	77	10	12	76.1
1981	Kansas City	134	77	934	53	3	4	73.9
1982	Kansas City	93	49	665	51	3	2	77.3
1983	L.A. Rams	0	0	0	0	0	0	00.0
1984	Chicago	78	53	595	31	3	0	103.3
1985	Chicago	107	53	777	69	1	5	57.3
Totals		**1,002**	**571**	**6,705**	**77**	**26**	**37**	**70.7**

GAJAN, Hokie NEW ORLEANS SAINTS
Position: Running Back; **Birthdate:** 06.09.59
College: Louisiana State; **Height:** 5–11; **Weight:** 226; **NFL Years:** 4

		RUSHING					RECEIVING				
Year	Club	Att.	Yds.	Avg.	Lg.	TDs	No.	Yds.	Avg.	Lg.	TDs
1981	New Orleans					Did not play					
1982	New Orleans	19	77	4.1	12	0	3	10	3.3	9	0
1983	New Orleans	81	415	5.1	58	4	17	130	7.6	26	0
1984	New Orleans	102	615	6.0	62t	5	35	288	8.2	51	2
1985	New Orleans	50	251	5.0	26	2	8	87	10.9	22	0
Totals		**252**	**1,358**	**5.4**	**62t**	**11**	**63**	**515**	**8.2**	**51**	**2**

GARRITY, Gregg PHILADELPHIA EAGLES
Position: Wide Receiver; **Birthdate:** 24.11.60
College: Penn State; **Height:** 5–10; **Weight:** 171; **NFL Years:** 3

		RECEIVING				
Year	Club	No.	Yds.	Avg.	Lg.	TDs
1983	Pittsburgh	19	279	14.7	38	1
1984	Pitt.–Phil.	2	22	11.0	12	0
1985	Philadelphia	7	142	20.3	34	0
Totals		**28**	**443**	**15.8**	**34**	**1**

WILLIE GAULT

DENNIS GENTRY

GALBREATH, Tony NEW YORK GIANTS
Position: Running Back; **Birthdate:** 29.01.54
College: Missouri; **Height:** 6–0; **Weight:** 228; **NFL Years:** 10

		RUSHING					RECEIVING				
Year	Club	Att.	Yds.	Avg.	Lg.	TDs	No.	Yds.	Avg.	Lg.	TDs
1976	New Orleans	136	570	4.2	74t	7	54	420	7.8	35	1
1977	New Orleans	168	644	3.8	26	3	41	265	6.5	30	0
1978	New Orleans	186	635	3.4	20t	5	74	582	7.9	35	2
1979	New Orleans	189	708	3.7	27	9	58	484	8.3	38	1
1980	New Orleans	81	308	3.8	26	3	57	470	8.2	21	2
1981	Minnesota	42	198	4.7	21	2	18	144	8.0	23	0
1982	Minnesota	39	116	3.0	12	1	17	153	9.0	32	0
1983	Minnesota	113	474	4.2	52t	4	45	348	7.7	23	2
1984	N.Y. Giants	22	97	4.4	11	0	37	357	9.6	37	0
1985	N.Y. Giants	29	187	6.4	18	0	30	327	10.9	49	1
Totals		**1,005**	**3,937**	**3.9**	**74t**	**34**	**431**	**3,550**	**8.2**	**49**	**9**

GAULT, Willie CHICAGO BEARS
Position: Wide Receiver; **Birthdate:** 05.09.60
College: Tennessee; **Height:** 6–1; **Weight:** 183; **NFL Years:** 3

		RECEIVING			
Year	Club	No.	Yds.	Avg.	Lg.	TDs
1983	Chicago	40	836	20.9	87t	8
1984	Chicago	34	587	17.3	61t	6
1985	Chicago	33	704	21.3	70t	1
Totals		**107**	**2,127**	**19.9**	**87t**	**15**

GENTRY, Dennis CHICAGO BEARS
Position: Running Back; **Birthdate:** 10.02.59
College: Baylor; **Height:** 5–8; **Weight:** 181; **NFL Years:** 4

		RUSHING					RECEIVING				
Year	Club	Att.	Yds.	Avg.	Lg.	TDs	No.	Yds.	Avg.	Lg.	TDs
1982	Chicago	4	21	5.3	9	0	1	9	9.0	9	0
1983	Chicago	16	65	4.1	17	0	2	8	4.0	6	0
1984	Chicago	21	79	3.8	28	1	4	29	7.3	13	0
1985	Chicago	30	160	5.3	21	2	5	77	15.4	30	0
Totals		**71**	**325**	**4.6**	**28**	**3**	**12**	**123**	**10.3**	**30**	**0**

GILBERT, Gale SEATTLE SEAHAWKS
Position: Quarterback; **Birthdate:** 20.12.61
College: California; **Height:** 6–3; **Weight:** 215; **NFL Years:** 1

			PASSING					
Year	**Club**	**Att.**	**Comp.**	**Yds.**	**Lg.**	**TDs**	**Int.**	**Rat.**
1985	Seattle	40	19	218	37t	1	2	51.9
Totals		**40**	**19**	**218**	**37t**	**1**	**2**	**51.9**

GILES, Jimmie TAMPA BAY BUCCANEERS
Position: Tight End; **Birthdate:** 08.11.54
College: Alcorn State; **Height:** 6–3; **Weight:** 240; **NFL Years:** 9

		RECEIVING				
Year	**Club**	**No.**	**Yds.**	**Avg.**	**Lg.**	**TDs**
1977	Houston	17	147	8.6	17	0
1978	Tampa Bay	23	324	14.1	38	2
1979	Tampa Bay	40	579	14.5	66t	7
1980	Tampa Bay	33	602	18.2	51	4
1981	Tampa Bay	45	786	17.5	81t	6
1982	Tampa Bay	28	499	17.8	48	3
1983	Tampa Bay	25	349	14.0	80	1
1984	Tampa Bay	24	310	12.9	38	2
1985	Tampa Bay	43	673	15.7	44	8
Totals		**278**	**4,269**	**15.4**	**81t**	**33**

GILL, Owen INDIANAPOLIS COLTS
Position: Running Back; **Birthdate:** 19.02.62
College: Iowa; **Height:** 6–1; **Weight:** 230; **NFL Years:** 1

		RUSHING					RECEIVING				
Year	**Club**	**Att.**	**Yds.**	**Avg.**	**Lg.**	**TDs**	**No.**	**Yds.**	**Avg.**	**Lg.**	**TDs**
1985	Indianapolis	45	262	5.8	67	2	5	52	10.4	20	0
Totals		**45**	**262**	**5.8**	**67**	**2**	**5**	**52**	**10.4**	**20**	**0**

GOODLOW, Eugene NEW ORLEANS SAINTS
Position: Wide Receiver; **Birthdate:** 19.12.58
College: Kansas State; **Height:** 6–2; **Weight:** 181; **NFL Years:** 3

		RECEIVING				
Year	**Club**	**No.**	**Yds.**	**Avg.**	**Lg.**	**TDs**
1983	New Orleans	41	487	11.9	26	2
1984	New Orleans	22	281	12.8	23	3
1985	New Orleans	32	603	18.8	76t	3
Totals		**95**	**1,371**	**14.4**	**76t**	**8**

GOTHARD, Preston PITTSBURGH STEELERS
Position: Tight End; **Birthdate:** 23.02.62
College: Alabama; **Height:** 6–4; **Weight:** 235; **NFL Years:** 1

		RECEIVING				
Year	**Club**	**No.**	**Yds.**	**Avg.**	**Lg.**	**TDs**
1985	Pittsburgh	6	83	13.8	24	0
Totals		**6**	**83**	**13.8**	**24**	**0**

JIMMIE GILES

EUGENE GOODLOW

79

GRAY, Earnest ST. LOUIS CARDINALS
Position: Wide Receiver; **Birthdate:** 02.03.57
College: Memphis State; **Height:** 6–3; **Weight:** 191; **NFL Years:** 7

		RECEIVING				
Year	Club	No.	Yds.	Avg.	Lg.	TDs
1979	N.Y. Giants	28	537	19.2	53t	4
1980	N.Y. Giants	52	777	14.9	50t	10
1981	N.Y. Giants	22	360	16.4	45	2
1982	N.Y. Giants	25	426	17.0	47	4
1983	N.Y. Giants	78	1,139	14.6	62	5
1984	N.Y. Giants	38	529	13.9	31	2
1985	N.Y.–St. Lou.	3	22	7.3	12	0
Totals		**246**	**3,790**	**15.4**	**62**	**27**

GREEN, Boyce KANSAS CITY CHIEFS
Position: Running Back; **Birthdate:** 24.06.60
College: Carson-Newman; **Height:** 5–11; **Weight:** 215; **NFL Years:** 3

		RUSHING					RECEIVING				
Year	Club	Att.	Yds.	Avg.	Lg.	TDs	No.	Yds.	Avg.	Lg.	TDs
1983	Cleveland	104	497	4.8	29	3	25	167	6.7	33	1
1984	Cleveland	202	673	3.3	29	0	12	124	10.3	44t	1
1985	Cleveland	0	0	0.0	0	0	0	0	0.0	0	0
Totals		**306**	**1,170**	**3.8**	**29**	**3**	**37**	**291**	**7.9**	**44t**	**2**

GREEN, Roy ST. LOUIS CARDINALS
Position: Wide Receiver; **Birthdate:** 30.06.57
College: Henderson State; **Height:** 6–0; **Weight:** 195; **NFL Years:** 7

		RECEIVING				
Year	Club	No.	Yds.	Avg.	Lg.	TDs
1979	St. Louis	1	15	15.0	15	0
1980	St. Louis	0	0	0.0	0	0
1981	St. Louis	33	708	21.5	60	4
1982	St. Louis	32	453	14.2	42	3
1983	St. Louis	78	1,227	15.7	71t	14
1984	St. Louis	78	1,555	19.9	83t	12
1985	St. Louis	50	693	13.9	47	5
Totals		**272**	**4,651**	**17.1**	**83t**	**38**

BOYCE GREEN

ROY GREEN

GREENE, Danny SEATTLE SEAHAWKS
Position: Wide Receiver; **Birthdate:** 26.12.61
College: Washington; **Height:** 5–11; **Weight:** 195; **NFL Years:** 1

		RECEIVING				
Year	Club	No.	Yds.	Avg.	Lg.	TDs
1985	Seattle	2	10	5.0	7	1
Totals		**2**	**10**	**5.0**	**7**	**1**

GRIFFIN, Keith WASHINGTON REDSKINS
Position: Running Back; **Birthdate:** 26.10.61
College: Miami; **Height:** 5–8; **Weight:** 185; **NFL Years:** 2

		RUSHING					RECEIVING				
Year	Club	Att.	Yds.	Avg.	Lg.	TDs	No.	Yds.	Avg.	Lg.	TDs
1984	Washington	97	408	4.2	31	0	8	43	5.4	8	0
1985	Washington	102	473	4.6	66t	3	37	285	7.7	28	0
Totals		**199**	**881**	**4.4**	**66t**	**3**	**45**	**328**	**7.3**	**28**	**0**

81

GROGAN, Steve NEW ENGLAND PATRIOTS
Position: Quarterback; **Birthdate:** 24.07.53
College: Kansas State; **Height:** 6–4; **Weight:** 210; **NFL Years:** 11

				PASSING				
Year	Club	Att.	Comp.	Yds.	Lg.	TDs	Int.	Rat.
1975	New England	274	139	1,976	62t	11	18	60.2
1976	New England	302	145	1,903	58t	18	20	60.8
1977	New England	305	160	2,162	68	17	21	65.3
1978	New England	362	181	2,824	75t	15	23	63.3
1979	New England	423	206	3,286	63t	28	20	77.5
1980	New England	306	175	2,475	71	18	22	73.1
1981	New England	216	117	1,859	76t	7	16	63.0
1982	New England	122	66	930	62t	7	4	84.2
1983	New England	303	168	2,411	76t	15	12	81.4
1984	New England	68	32	444	65t	3	6	46.4
1985	New England	156	85	1,311	56	7	5	84.1
Totals		**2,837**	**1,474**	**21,581**	**76t**	**146**	**167**	**69.7**

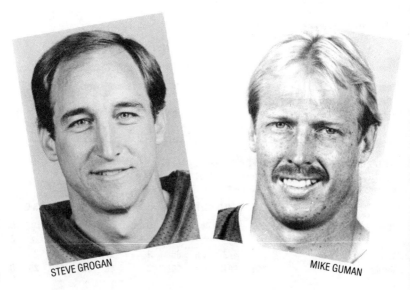

STEVE GROGAN

MIKE GUMAN

GROTH, Jeff NEW ORLEANS SAINTS
Position: Wide Receiver; **Birthdate:** 02.07.57
College: Bowling Green; **Height:** 5–10; **Weight:** 181; **NFL Years:** 7

		RECEIVING				
Year	Club	No.	Yds.	Avg.	Lg.	TDs
1979	Mia.–Hou.	1	6	6.0	6	0
1980	Houston	4	47	11.8	18	0
1981	New Orleans	20	380	19.0	54	1
1982	New Orleans	30	383	12.8	39	1
1983	New Orleans	49	585	11.9	42	1
1984	New Orleans	33	487	14.8	31	0
1985	New Orleans	15	238	15.9	56t	2
Totals		**152**	**2,126**	**14.0**	**56t**	**5**

GUMAN, Mike LOS ANGELES RAMS
Position: Running Back; **Birthdate:** 21.04.58
College: Penn State; **Height:** 6–2; **Weight:** 218; **NFL Years:** 6

		RUSHING					RECEIVING				
Year	Club	Att.	Yds.	Avg.	Lg.	TDs	No.	Yds.	Avg.	Lg.	TDs
1980	L.A. Rams	100	410	4.1	17	4	14	131	9.4	41	0
1981	L.A. Rams	115	433	3.8	18	4	18	130	7.2	14	0
1982	L.A. Rams	69	266	3.9	15	2	31	310	10.0	46	0
1983	L.A. Rams	7	42	6.0	11	0	34	347	10.2	60	4
1984	L.A. Rams	1	2	2.0	2	0	19	161	8.5	29	0
1985	L.A. Rams	11	32	2.9	6	0	3	23	7.7	11	0
Totals		**303**	**1,185**	**3.9**	**18**	**10**	**119**	**1,102**	**9.3**	**60**	**4**

HADDIX, Michael PHILADELPHIA EAGLES
Position: Running Back; **Birthdate:** 27.12.61
College: Mississippi State; **Height:** 6–2; **Weight:** 225; **NFL Years:** 3

		RUSHING					RECEIVING				
Year	Club	Att.	Yds.	Avg.	Lg.	TDs	No.	Yds.	Avg.	Lg.	TDs
1983	Philadelphia	91	220	2.4	11	2	23	254	11.0	34	0
1984	Philadelphia	48	130	2.7	21	1	33	231	7.0	22	0
1985	Philadelphia	67	213	3.2	12	0	43	330	7.7	17	0
Totals		**206**	**563**	**2.7**	**21**	**3**	**99**	**815**	**8.2**	**34**	**0**

HAJI-SHEIKH, Ali NEW YORK GIANTS
Position: Placekicker; **Birthdate:** 11.01.61
College: Michigan; **Height:** 6–0; **Weight:** 170; **NFL Years:** 2

		SCORING					
Year	Club	EPA	EPM	FGA	FGM	Lg.	Pts.
1983	N.Y. Giants	23	22	42	35	56	127
1984	N.Y. Giants	35	32	33	17	48	83
1985	N.Y. Giants	5	5	5	2	52	11
Totals		**63**	**59**	**80**	**54**	**56**	**221**

HAMPTON, Lorenzo MIAMI DOLPHINS
Position: Running Back; **Birthdate:** 12.03.62
College: Florida; **Height:** 6–0; **Weight:** 212; **NFL Years:** 1

		RUSHING					RECEIVING				
Year	Club	Att.	Yds.	Avg.	Lg.	TDs	No.	Yds.	Avg.	Lg.	TDs
1985	Miami	105	369	3.5	15	3	8	56	7.0	15	0
Totals		**105**	**369**	**3.5**	**15**	**3**	**8**	**56**	**7.0**	**15**	**0**

HANCOCK, Anthony KANSAS CITY CHIEFS
Position: Wide Receiver; **Birthdate:** 10.06.60
College: Tennessee; **Height:** 6–0; **Weight:** 204; **NFL Years:** 4

		RECEIVING			
Year	Club	No.	Yds.	Avg.	Lg.	TDs
1982	Kansas City	7	116	16.6	41t	1
1983	Kansas City	37	584	15.8	50	1
1984	Kansas City	10	217	21.7	46t	1
1985	Kansas City	15	286	19.1	48	2
Totals		**69**	**1,203**	**17.4**	**50**	**5**

HARDY, Bruce MIAMI DOLPHINS
Position: Tight End; **Birthdate:** 01.06.56
College: Arizona State; **Height:** 6–5; **Weight:** 232; **NFL Years:** 8

		RECEIVING				
Year	Club	No.	Yds.	Avg.	Lg.	TDs
1978	Miami	4	32	8.0	15	2
1979	Miami	30	386	12.9	28	3
1980	Miami	19	159	8.4	19	2
1981	Miami	15	174	11.6	21	0
1982	Miami	12	66	5.5	19	2
1983	Miami	22	202	9.2	25	0
1984	Miami	28	257	9.2	19	5
1985	Miami	39	409	10.5	31	4
Totals		**169**	**1,685**	**10.0**	**31**	**18**

ANTHONY HANCOCK

BRUCE HARDY

85

HARDY, Larry NEW ORLEANS SAINTS
Position: Tight End; **Birthdate:** 09.07.56
College: Jackson State; **Height:** 6–3; **Weight:** 246; **NFL Years:** 8

		RECEIVING				
Year	Club	No.	Yds.	Avg.	Lg.	TDs
1978	New Orleans	5	131	26.2	71t	1
1979	New Orleans	1	3	3.0	3t	1
1980	New Orleans	13	197	15.2	44	0
1981	New Orleans	23	275	12.0	27	1
1982	New Orleans	8	67	8.4	31	1
1983	New Orleans	2	29	14.5	22	0
1984	New Orleans	4	50	12.5	28t	1
1985	New Orleans	15	208	13.9	31	2
Totals		**71**	**960**	**13.5**	**71t**	**7**

HARMON, Derrick SAN FRANCISCO 49ers
Position: Running Back; **Birthdate:** 26.04.63
College: Cornell; **Height:** 5–10; **Weight:** 202; **NFL Years:** 2

		RUSHING					RECEIVING				
Year	Club	Att.	Yds.	Avg.	Lg.	TDs	No.	Yds.	Avg.	Lg.	TDs
1984	San Francisco	39	192	4.9	19	1	1	2	2.0	2	0
1985	San Francisco	28	92	3.3	17	0	14	123	8.8	42	0
Totals		**67**	**284**	**4.2**	**19**	**1**	**15**	**125**	**8.3**	**42**	**0**

HARRINGTON, Perry ST. LOUIS CARDINALS
Position: Running Back; **Birthdate:** 13.03.58
College: Jackson State; **Height:** 5–11; **Weight:** 216; **NFL Years:** 6

		RUSHING					RECEIVING				
Year	Club	Att.	Yds.	Avg.	Lg.	TDs	No.	Yds.	Avg.	Lg.	TDs
1980	Philadelphia	32	166	5.2	19t	1	3	24	8.0	17	0
1981	Philadelphia	34	140	4.1	16	2	9	27	3.0	12	0
1982	Philadelphia	56	231	4.1	37	1	13	74	5.7	18	0
1983	Philadelphia	23	98	4.3	35	1	1	19	19.0	19	0
1984	St. Louis	3	6	2.0	5	0	0	0	0.0	0	0
1985	St. Louis	7	42	6.0	22	1	0	0	0.0	0	0
Totals		**155**	**683**	**4.4**	**37**	**6**	**26**	**144**	**5.5**	**19**	**0**

HARRIS, M.L. CINCINNATI BENGALS
Position: Tight End; **Birthdate:** 16.01.54
College: Kansas State; **Height:** 6–5; **Weight:** 238; **NFL Years:** 6

		RECEIVING				
Year	**Club**	**No.**	**Yds.**	**Avg.**	**Lg.**	**TDs**
1980	Cincinnati	10	137	13.7	26	0
1981	Cincinnati	13	181	13.9	42	2
1982	Cincinnati	10	103	10.3	17t	3
1983	Cincinnati	8	66	8.3	14	2
1984	Cincinnati	48	759	15.8	80t	2
1985	Cincinnati	10	123	12.3	22t	1
Totals		**99**	**1,369**	**13.8**	**80t**	**10**

LARRY HARDY   M. L. HARRIS

HASSELBECK, Don NEW YORK GIANTS
Position: Tight End; **Birthdate:** 01.04.55
College: Colorado; **Height:** 6–7; **Weight:** 245; **NFL Years:** 9

		RECEIVING				
Year	Club	No.	Yds.	Avg.	Lg.	TDs
1977	New England	9	76	8.4	21	4
1978	New England	7	107	15.3	24	0
1979	New England	13	158	12.2	41	0
1980	New England	8	130	16.3	35t	4
1981	New England	46	808	17.6	51	6
1982	New England	15	158	10.5	41	1
1983	N.E.–Raiders	3	24	8.0	13t	2
1984	Minnesota	1	10	10.0	10	0
1985	N.Y. Giants	5	71	14.2	30	1
Totals		**107**	**1,542**	**14.4**	**51**	**18**

HAWKINS, Frank LOS ANGELES RAIDERS
Position: Running Back; **Birthdate:** 03.07.59
College: Nevada-Reno; **Height:** 5–9; **Weight:** 210; **NFL Years:** 5

		RUSHING					RECEIVING				
Year	Club	Att.	Yds.	Avg.	Lg.	TDs	No.	Yds.	Avg.	Lg.	TDs
1981	Oakland	40	165	4.1	19	0	10	109	10.9	35	0
1982	L.A. Raiders	27	54	2.0	11	2	7	35	5.0	9	1
1983	L.A. Raiders	110	526	4.8	32	6	20	150	7.5	28	2

FRANK HAWKINS

GREG HAWTHORNE

Year	Club	Att.	Yds.	Avg.	Lg.	TDs	No.	Yds.	Avg.	Lg.	TDs
1984	L.A. Raiders	108	376	3.5	17	3	7	51	7.3	15	0
1985	L.A. Raiders	84	269	3.2	21t	4	27	174	6.4	20	0
Totals		**369**	**1,390**	**3.8**	**32**	**15**	**71**	**519**	**7.3**	**35**	**3**

HAWTHORNE, Greg NEW ENGLAND PATRIOTS
Position: Running Back – Wide Receiver; **Birthdate:** 05.09.56
College: Baylor; **Height:** 6–3; **Weight:** 225; **NFL Years:** 7

Year	Club	RUSHING					RECEIVING				
		Att.	Yds.	Avg.	Lg.	TDs	No.	Yds.	Avg.	Lg.	TDs
1979	Pittsburgh	28	123	4.4	19	1	8	47	5.9	17	0
1980	Pittsburgh	63	226	3.6	15	4	12	158	13.2	33	0
1981	Pittsburgh	25	58	2.3	16	2	4	23	5.8	12	0
1982	Pittsburgh	15	68	4.5	11	0	12	182	15.2	46t	3
1983	Pittsburgh	5	47	9.4	20	0	19	300	15.8	52	0
1984	New England	0	0	0.0	0	0	7	127	18.1	26	0
1985	New England	0	0	0.0	0	0	3	42	14.0	28t	1
Totals		**136**	**522**	**3.8**	**20**	**7**	**65**	**879**	**13.5**	**52**	**4**

HAYES, Jonathan KANSAS CITY CHIEFS
Position: Tight End; **Birthdate:** 11.08.62
College: Iowa; **Height:** 6–5; **Weight:** 234; **NFL Years:** 1

Year	Club	RECEIVING				
		No.	Yds.	Avg.	Lg.	TDs
1985	Kansas City	5	39	7.8	12	1
Totals		**5**	**39**	**7.8**	**12**	**1**

HEARD, Herman KANSAS CITY CHIEFS
Position: Running Back; **Birthdate:** 24.11.61
College: Southern Colorado; **Height:** 5–10; **Weight:** 184; **NFL Years:** 2

Year	Club	RUSHING					RECEIVING				
		Att.	Yds.	Avg.	Lg.	TDs	No.	Yds.	Avg.	Lg.	TDs
1984	Kansas City	165	684	4.1	69t	4	25	223	8.9	17	0
1985	Kansas City	164	595	3.6	33	4	31	257	8.3	27	2
Totals		**329**	**1,279**	**3.9**	**69t**	**8**	**56**	**480**	**8.6**	**27**	**2**

JESSIE HESTER

DAVID HILL

HEBERT, Bobby NEW ORLEANS SAINTS
Position: Quarterback; **Birthdate:** 19.08.60
College: N.W. Louisiana State; **Height:** 6–4; **Weight:** 208; **NFL Years:** 1

		PASSING						
Year	Club	Att.	Comp.	Yds.	Lg.	TDs	Int.	Rat.
1985	New Orleans	181	97	1,208	76t	5	4	74.6
Totals		**181**	**97**	**1,208**	**76t**	**5**	**4**	**74.6**

HECTOR, Johnny NEW YORK JETS
Position: Running Back; **Birthdate:** 26.11.60
College: Texas A&M; **Height:** 5–11; **Weight:** 197; **NFL Years:** 3

		RUSHING					RECEIVING				
Year	Club	Att.	Yds.	Avg.	Lg.	TDs	No.	Yds.	Avg.	Lg.	TDs
1983	N.Y. Jets	16	85	5.3	42	0	5	61	12.2	22t	1
1984	N.Y. Jets	124	531	4.3	64	1	20	182	9.1	26	0
1985	N.Y. Jets	145	572	3.9	22	6	17	164	9.6	28	0
Totals		**285**	**1,188**	**4.2**	**64**	**7**	**42**	**407**	**9.7**	**28**	**1**

HEFLIN, Vince MIAMI DOLPHINS
Position: Wide Receiver; **Birthdate:** 07.07.59
College: Central State (Ohio); **Height:** 6–0; **Weight:** 185; **NFL Years:** 4

		RECEIVING			
Year	Club	No.	Yds.	Avg.	Lg.	TDs
1982	Miami	0	0	0.0	0	0

Year	Club	No.	Yds.	Avg.	Lg.	TDs
1983	Miami	0	0	0.0	0	0
1984	Miami	0	0	0.0	0	0
1985	Miami	6	98	16.3	46t	1
Totals		**6**	**98**	**16.3**	**46t**	**1**

HERRMANN, Mark SAN DIEGO CHARGERS
Position: Quarterback; **Birthdate:** 08.01.59
College: Purdue; **Height:** 6–4; **Weight:** 209; **NFL Years:** 5

				PASSING				
Year	Club	Att.	Comp.	Yds.	Lg.	TDs	Int.	Rat.
1981	Denver	0	0	0	0	0	0	00.0
1982	Denver	60	32	421	39	1	4	53.5
1983	Baltimore	36	18	256	35	0	3	38.7
1984	Indianapolis	56	29	352	74t	1	6	37.8
1985	San Diego	201	132	1,537	59	10	10	84.5
Totals		**353**	**211**	**2,566**	**74t**	**12**	**23**	**66.4**

HESTER, Jessie LOS ANGELES RAIDERS
Position: Wide Receiver; **Birthdate:** 21.01.63
College: Florida State; **Height:** 5–11; **Weight:** 170; **NFL Years:** 1

				RECEIVING		
Year	Club	No.	Yds.	Avg.	Lg.	TDs
1985	L.A. Raiders	32	665	20.8	59	4
Totals		**32**	**665**	**20.8**	**59**	**4**

HILL, David LOS ANGELES RAMS
Position: Tight End; **Birthdate:** 01.01.54
College: Texas A&I; **Height:** 6–2; **Weight:** 240; **NFL Years:** 10

				RECEIVING		
Year	Club	No.	Yds.	Avg.	Lg.	TDs
1976	Detroit	19	249	13.1	24t	5
1977	Detroit	32	465	14.5	61	2
1978	Detroit	53	633	11.9	32	4
1979	Detroit	47	569	12.1	40	3
1980	Detroit	39	424	10.9	29	1

Year	Club	No.	Yds.	Avg.	Lg.	TDs
1981	Detroit	33	462	14.0	34	4
1982	Detroit	22	252	11.5	27	4
1983	L.A. Rams	28	280	10.0	34	2
1984	L.A. Rams	31	300	9.7	26	1
1985	L.A. Rams	29	271	9.3	37	1
Totals		**333**	**3,905**	**11.7**	**61**	**27**

HILL, Drew HOUSTON OILERS
Position: Wide Receiver; **Birthdate:** 05.10.56
College: Georgia Tech; **Height:** 5–9; **Weight:** 170; **NFL Years:** 6

		RECEIVING				
Year	Club	No.	Yds.	Avg.	Lg.	TDs
1979	L.A. Rams	4	94	23.5	43	1
1980	L.A. Rams	19	416	21.9	74t	2
1981	L.A. Rams	16	355	22.2	45	3
1982	L.A. Rams	7	92	13.1	23	0
1983	L.A. Rams			Did not play		
1984	L.A. Rams	14	390	27.9	68	4
1985	Houston	64	1,169	18.3	57t	9
Totals		**124**	**2,516**	**20.3**	**74t**	**19**

HILL, Tony DALLAS COWBOYS
Position: Wide Receiver; **Birthdate:** 23.06.56
College: Stanford; **Height:** 6–2; **Weight:** 202; **NFL Years:** 9

		RECEIVING				
Year	Club	No.	Yds.	Avg.	Lg.	TDs
1977	Dallas	2	21	10.5	12	0
1978	Dallas	46	823	17.9	54	6
1979	Dallas	60	1,062	17.7	75t	10
1980	Dallas	60	1,055	17.6	58t	8
1981	Dallas	46	953	20.7	63t	4
1982	Dallas	35	526	15.0	47	1
1983	Dallas	49	801	16.3	75t	7
1984	Dallas	58	864	14.9	66t	5
1985	Dallas	74	1,113	15.0	53t	7
Totals		**430**	**7,218**	**16.8**	**75t**	**48**

DREW HILL

ERIC HIPPLE

HIPPLE, Eric DETROIT LIONS
Position: Quarterback; **Birthdate:** 16.09.57
College: Utah State; **Height:** 6–2; **Weight:** 198; **NFL Years:** 6

		PASSING						
Year	Club	Att.	Comp.	Yds.	Lg.	TDs	Int.	Rat.
1980	Detroit	0	0	0	0	0	0	00.0
1981	Detroit	279	140	2,358	94t	14	15	73.3
1982	Detroit	86	36	411	52	2	4	45.0
1983	Detroit	387	204	2,577	80t	12	18	64.7
1984	Detroit	38	16	246	40	1	1	62.0
1985	Detroit	406	223	2,952	56	17	18	73.6
Totals		**1,196**	**619**	**8,544**	**94t**	**46**	**56**	**68.3**

HOGEBOOM, Gary INDIANAPOLIS COLTS
Position: Quarterback; **Birthdate:** 21.08.58
College: Central Michigan; **Height:** 6–4; **Weight:** 207; **NFL Years:** 6

		PASSING						
Year	Club	Att.	Comp.	Yds.	Lg.	TDs	Int.	Rat.
1980	Dallas	0	0	0	0	0	0	00.0
1981	Dallas	0	0	0	0	0	0	00.0
1982	Dallas	8	3	45	26	0	1	17.2
1983	Dallas	17	11	161	24	1	1	90.6
1984	Dallas	367	195	2,366	68t	7	14	63.7
1985	Dallas	126	70	978	58t	5	7	70.8
Totals		**518**	**279**	**3,550**	**68t**	**13**	**23**	**65.4**

HOLMAN, Rodney CINCINNATI BENGALS
Position: Tight End; **Birthdate:** 20.04.60
College: Tulane; **Height:** 6–3; **Weight:** 232; **NFL Years:** 4

		RECEIVING				
Year	**Club**	**No.**	**Yds.**	**Avg.**	**Lg.**	**TDs**
1982	Cincinnati	3	18	6.0	10	1
1983	Cincinnati	2	15	7.5	10	0
1984	Cincinnati	21	239	11.4	27	1
1985	Cincinnati	38	479	12.6	64t	7
Totals		**64**	**751**	**11.7**	**64t**	**9**

HOLOHAN, Pete SAN DIEGO CHARGERS
Position: Tight End; **Birthdate:** 25.07.59
College: Notre Dame; **Height:** 6–4; **Weight:** 244; **NFL Years:** 5

		RECEIVING				
Year	**Club**	**No.**	**Yds.**	**Avg.**	**Lg.**	**TDs**
1981	San Diego	1	14	14.0	14	0
1982	San Diego	0	0	0.0	0	0
1983	San Diego	23	272	11.8	35	2
1984	San Diego	56	734	13.1	51	1
1985	San Diego	42	458	10.9	23	3
Totals		**122**	**1,478**	**12.1**	**51**	**6**

HOLT, Harry CLEVELAND BROWNS
Position: Tight End; **Birthdate:** 29.12.57
College: Arizona; **Height:** 6–4; **Weight:** 230; **NFL Years:** 3

		RECEIVING				
Year	**Club**	**No.**	**Yds.**	**Avg.**	**Lg.**	**TDs**
1983	Cleveland	29	420	14.5	48t	3
1984	Cleveland	20	261	13.1	36	0
1985	Cleveland	10	95	9.5	23	1
94 **Totals**		**59**	**776**	**13.2**	**48t**	**4**

HORTON, Ethan KANSAS CITY CHIEFS
Position: Running Back; **Birthdate:** 19.12.62
College: North Carolina; **Height:** 6–3; **Weight:** 228; **NFL Years:** 1

Year	Club	Att.	Yds.	Avg.	Lg.	TDs	No.	Yds.	Avg.	Lg.	TDs
			RUSHING					**RECEIVING**			
1985	Kansas City	48	146	3.0	19t	3	28	185	6.6	22	1
Totals		**48**	**146**	**3.0**	**19t**	**3**	**28**	**185**	**6.6**	**22**	**1**

HOSTETLER, Jeff NEW YORK GIANTS
Position: Quarterback; **Birthdate:** 22.04.61
College: West Virginia; **Height:** 6–3; **Weight:** 212; **NFL Years:** 2

Year	Club	Att.	Comp.	Yds.	Lg.	TDs	Int.	Rat.
				PASSING				
1984	N.Y. Giants	0	0	0	0	0	0	00 0
1985	N.Y. Giants	0	0	0	0	0	0	00.0
Totals		**0**	**0**	**0**	**0**	**0**	**0**	**00.0**

RODNEY HOLMAN

PETE HOLOHAN

HOUSE, Kevin TAMPA BAY BUCCANEERS
Position: Wide Receiver; **Birthdate:** 20.12.57
College: Southern Illinois; **Height:** 6–1; **Weight:** 185; **NFL Years:** 6

		RECEIVING				
Year	Club	No.	Yds.	Avg.	Lg.	TDs
1980	Tampa Bay	24	531	22.1	61	5
1981	Tampa Bay	56	1,176	21.0	84t	9
1982	Tampa Bay	28	438	15.6	62t	2
1983	Tampa Bay	47	769	16.4	74t	5
1984	Tampa Bay	76	1,005	13.2	55	5
1985	Tampa Bay	44	803	18.3	59	5
Totals		**275**	**4,722**	**17.2**	**84t**	**31**

HUCKLEBY, Harlan GREEN BAY PACKERS
Position: Running Back; **Birthdate:** 30.12.57
College: Michigan; **Height:** 6–1; **Weight:** 201; **NFL Years:** 6

		RUSHING					RECEIVING				
Year	Club	Att.	Yds.	Avg.	Lg.	TDs	No.	Yds.	Avg.	Lg.	TDs
1980	Green Bay	6	11	1.8	9	1	3	11	3.7	8	0
1981	Green Bay	139	381	2.7	22	5	27	221	8.2	39t	3
1982	Green Bay	4	19	4.8	7	0	0	0	0.0	0	0
1983	Green Bay	50	182	3.6	20	4	10	87	8.7	14	0
1984	Green Bay	35	145	4.1	23	0	8	65	8.1	13	0
1985	Green Bay	8	41	5.1	15	0	5	27	5.4	8	0
Totals		**242**	**779**	**3.2**	**23**	**10**	**53**	**411**	**7.8**	**39t**	**3**

HUGHES, David SEATTLE SEAHAWKS
Position: Running Back; **Birthdate:** 01.06.59
College: Boise State; **Height:** 6–0; **Weight:** 220; **NFL Years:** 5

		RUSHING					RECEIVING				
Year	Club	Att.	Yds.	Avg.	Lg.	TDs	No.	Yds.	Avg.	Lg.	TDs
1981	Seattle	47	135	2.9	15	0	35	263	7.5	22	2
1982	Seattle	30	106	3.5	13	0	11	98	8.9	29t	1
1983	Seattle	83	313	3.8	26	1	10	100	10.0	33t	1
1984	Seattle	94	327	3.5	14	1	22	121	5.5	25	1
1985	Seattle	40	128	3.2	9	0	19	184	9.7	26	0
Totals		**294**	**1,009**	**3.4**	**26**	**2**	**97**	**766**	**7.9**	**33t**	**5**

KEVIN HOUSE

HERMAN HUNTER

HUMPHERY, Bobby NEW YORK JETS
Position: Wide Receiver; **Birthdate:** 23.08.61
College: New Mexico State; **Height:** 5–10; **Weight:** 180; **NFL Years:** 2

		RECEIVING				
Year	Club	No.	Yds.	Avg.	Lg.	TDs
1983	N.Y. Jets			Did not play		
1984	N.Y. Jets	14	206	14.7	44t	1
1985	N.Y. Jets	0	0	0.0	0	0
Totals		**14**	**206**	**14.7**	**44t**	**1**

HUNTER, Herman PHILADELPHIA EAGLES
Position: Running Back; **Birthdate:** 14.02.61
College: Tennessee State; **Height:** 6–1; **Weight:** 193; **NFL Years:** 1

		RUSHING					RECEIVING				
Year	Club	Att.	Yds.	Avg.	Lg.	TDs	No.	Yds.	Avg.	Lg.	TDs
1985	Philadelphia	27	121	4.5	74t	1	28	405	14.5	43	1
Totals		**27**	**121**	**4.5**	**74t**	**1**	**28**	**405**	**14.5**	**43**	**1**

HUNTER, Tony LOS ANGELES RAMS
Position: Tight End; **Birthdate:** 22.05.60
College: Notre Dame; **Height:** 6–4; **Weight:** 237; **NFL Years:** 3

		RECEIVING				
Year	Club	No.	Yds.	Avg.	Lg.	TDs
1983	Buffalo	36	402	11.2	40t	3
1984	Buffalo	33	331	10.0	30	2
1985	L.A. Rams	50	562	11.2	47t	4
Totals		**119**	**1,295**	**10.9**	**47t**	**9**

HUTCHISON, Anthony BUFFALO BILLS
Position: Running Back; **Birthdate:** 04.02.61
College: Texas Tech; **Height:** 5–10; **Weight:** 186; **NFL Years:** 3

		RUSHING					RECEIVING				
Year	Club	Att.	Yds.	Avg.	Lg.	TDs	No.	Yds.	Avg.	Lg.	TDs
1983	Chicago	6	13	2.2	5	1	0	0	0.0	0	0
1984	Chicago	14	39	2.8	6	1	1	7	7.0	7	0
1985	Buffalo	2	11	5.5	7	0	0	0	0.0	0	0
Totals		**22**	**63**	**2.9**	**7**	**2**	**1**	**7**	**7.0**	**7**	**0**

TONY HUNTER

DONALD IGWEBUIKE

IGWEBUIKE, Donald TAMPA BAY BUCCANEERS
Position: Placekicker; **Birthdate:** 27.12.60
College: Clemson; **Height:** 5–9; **Weight:** 185; **NFL Years:** 1

		SCORING					
Year	Club	EPA	EPM	FGA	FGM	Lg.	Pts.
1985	Tampa Bay	32	30	32	22	53	96
Totals		**32**	**30**	**32**	**22**	**53**	**96**

IVERY, Eddie Lee GREEN BAY PACKERS
Position: Running Back; **Birthdate:** 30.07.57
College: Georgia Tech; **Height:** 6–0; **Weight:** 214; **NFL Years:** 5

		RUSHING					RECEIVING				
Year	Club	Att.	Yds.	Avg.	Lg.	TDs	No.	Yds.	Avg.	Lg.	TDs
1979	Green Bay	3	24	8.0	11	0	0	0	0.0	0	0
1980	Green Bay	202	831	4.1	38t	3	50	481	9.6	46t	1
1981	Green Bay	14	72	5.1	28	1	2	10	5.0	8	0
1982	Green Bay	127	453	3.6	32	9	16	186	11.6	62	1
1983	Green Bay	86	340	4.0	21	2	16	139	8.7	17	1
1984	Green Bay	99	552	5.6	49	6	19	141	7.4	18	1
1985	Green Bay	132	636	4.8	34	2	28	270	9.6	24	2
Totals		**663**	**2,908**	**4.4**	**49**	**23**	**131**	**1,227**	**9.4**	**62**	**6**

JACKSON, Earnest PHILADELPHIA EAGLES
Position: Running Back; **Birthdate:** 18.12.59
College: Texas A&M; **Height:** 5–10; **Weight:** 206; **NFL Years:** 3

		RUSHING					RECEIVING				
Year	Club	Att.	Yds.	Avg.	Lg.	TDs	No.	Yds.	Avg.	Lg.	TDs
1983	San Diego	11	39	3.5	6	0	5	42	8.4	10	0
1984	San Diego	296	1,179	4.0	32t	8	39	222	5.7	21	1
1985	Philadelphia	282	1,028	3.6	59	5	10	126	12.6	25	1
Totals		**589**	**2,246**	**3.8**	**59**	**13**	**54**	**390**	**7.2**	**25**	**2**

JACKSON, Kenny PHILADELPHIA EAGLES
Position: Wide Receiver; **Birthdate:** 15.02.62
College: Penn State; **Height:** 6–0; **Weight:** 177; **NFL Years:** 2

		RECEIVING				
Year	Club	No.	Yds.	Avg.	Lg.	TDs
1984	Philadelphia	26	398	15.3	83t	1
1985	Philadelphia	40	692	17.3	54	1
Totals		**66**	**1,090**	**16.5**	**83t**	**2**

JAMES, Craig NEW ENGLAND PATRIOTS
Position: Running Back; **Birthdate:** 02.01.61
College: SMU; **Height:** 6–0; **Weight:** 215; **NFL Years:** 2

		RUSHING					RECEIVING				
Year	Club	Att.	Yds.	Avg.	Lg.	TDs	No.	Yds.	Avg.	Lg.	TDs
1984	New England	160	790	4.9	73	1	22	159	7.2	16	0
1985	New England	263	1,227	4.7	65t	5	27	360	13.3	90t	2
Totals		**423**	**2,017**	**4.8**	**73**	**6**	**49**	**519**	**10.6**	**90t**	**2**

JAMES, Lionel SAN DIEGO CHARGERS
Position: Running Back; **Birthdate:** 25.05.62
College: Auburn; **Height:** 5–6; **Weight:** 172; **NFL Years:** 2

		RUSHING					RECEIVING				
Year	Club	Att.	Yds.	Avg.	Lg.	TDs	No.	Yds.	Avg.	Lg.	TDs
1984	San Diego	25	115	4.6	20	0	23	206	9.0	31	0
1985	San Diego	105	516	4.9	56t	2	86	1,027	11.9	67t	6
Totals		**130**	**631**	**4.9**	**56t**	**2**	**109**	**1,233**	**11.3**	**67t**	**6**

JAWORSKI, Ron PHILADELPHIA EAGLES
Position: Quarterback; **Birthdate:** 23.03.51
College: Youngstown State; **Height:** 6–2; **Weight:** 199; **NFL Years:** 12

			PASSING					
Year	Club	Att.	Comp.	Yds.	Lg.	TDs	Int.	Rat.
1973	L.A. Rams			Did not play				
1974	L.A. Rams	24	10	144	22	0	1	44.3

Year	Club	Att.	Comp.	Yds.	Lg.	TDs	Int.	Rat.
1975	L.A. Rams	48	24	302	25	0	2	52.5
1976	L.A. Rams	52	20	273	42	1	5	22.8
1977	Philadelphia	346	166	2,183	55t	18	21	60.3
1978	Philadelphia	398	206	2,487	56t	16	16	68.0
1979	Philadelphia	374	190	2,669	53t	18	12	76.8
1980	Philadelphia	451	257	3,529	56t	27	12	90.9
1981	Philadelphia	461	250	3,095	85t	23	20	74.0
1982	Philadelphia	286	167	2,076	57	12	12	77.5
1983	Philadelphia	446	235	3,315	83t	20	18	75.1
1984	Philadelphia	427	234	2,754	90t	16	14	73.5
1985	Philadelphia	484	255	3,450	99t	17	20	70.2
Totals		**3,797**	**2,014**	**26,277**	**99t**	**168**	**153**	**73.1**

CRAIG JAMES

RON JAWORSKI

JEFFERSON, John HOUSTON OILERS
Position: Wide Receiver; **Birthdate:** 03.02.56
College: Arizona State; **Height:** 6–1; **Weight:** 204; **NFL Years:** 8

		RECEIVING				
Year	Club	No.	Yds.	Avg.	Lg.	TDs
1978	San Diego	56	1,001	17.9	46t	13
1979	San Diego	61	1,090	17.9	65t	10
1980	San Diego	82	1,340	16.3	58t	13
1981	Green Bay	39	632	16.2	41	4
1982	Green Bay	27	452	16.7	50	0
1983	Green Bay	57	830	14.6	36	7
1984	Green Bay	26	339	13.0	33	0
1985	Cleveland	3	30	10.0	17	0
Totals		**351**	**5,714**	**16.3**	**65t**	**47**

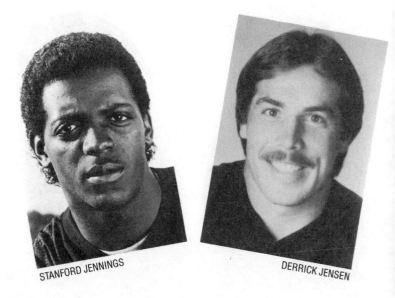

STANFORD JENNINGS

DERRICK JENSEN

JENKINS, Ken WASHINGTON REDSKINS
Position: Running Back; **Birthdate:** 08.05.59
College: Bucknell; **Height:** 5–8; **Weight:** 185; **NFL Years:** 3

		RUSHING					RECEIVING				
Year	Club	Att.	Yds.	Avg.	Lg.	TDs	No.	Yds.	Avg.	Lg.	TDs
1982	Philadelphia					Did not play					
1983	Detroit	0	0	0.0	0	0	0	0	0.0	0	0
1984	Detroit	78	358	4.6	25t	1	21	246	11.7	68	0
1985	Washington	2	39	19.5	37	0	0	0	0.0	0	0
Totals		**80**	**397**	**5.0**	**37**	**1**	**21**	**246**	**11.7**	**68**	**0**

JENNINGS, Stanford CINCINNATI BENGALS
Position: Running Back; **Birthdate:** 12.03.62
College: Furman; **Height:** 6–1; **Weight:** 205; **NFL Years:** 2

		RUSHING					RECEIVING				
Year	Club	Att.	Yds.	Avg.	Lg.	TDs	No.	Yds.	Avg.	Lg.	TDs
1984	Cincinnati	79	379	4.8	20t	2	35	346	9.9	43	3
1985	Cincinnati	31	92	3.0	19	1	12	101	8.4	24	3
Totals		**110**	**471**	**4.3**	**20t**	**3**	**47**	**447**	**9.5**	**43**	**6**

JENSEN, Derrick LOS ANGELES RAIDERS
Position: Running Back – Tight End; **Birthdate:** 27.04.56
College: Texas-Arlington; **Height:** 6–1; **Weight:** 220; **NFL Years:** 7

		RUSHING					RECEIVING				
Year	Club	Att.	Yds.	Avg.	Lg.	TDs	No.	Yds.	Avg.	Lg.	TDs
1978	Oakland					Did not play					
1979	Oakland	73	251	3.4	15	0	7	23	3.3	7	1
1980	Oakland	14	30	2.1	4	0	7	87	12.4	32	0
1981	Oakland	117	456	3.9	33	4	28	271	9.7	21	0
1982	L.A. Raiders	0	0	0.0	0	0	0	0	0.0	0	0
1983	L.A. Raiders	1	5	5.0	5	0	1	2	2.0	2t	1
1984	L.A. Raiders	3	3	1.0	2	1	1	1	1.0	1t	1
1985	L.A. Raiders	16	35	2.2	8	0	0	0	0.0	0	0
Totals		**224**	**780**	**3.5**	**33**	**5**	**44**	**384**	**8.7**	**32**	**3**

103

JENSEN, Jim MIAMI DOLPHINS
Position: Wide Receiver; **Birthdate:** 14.11.58
College: Boston University; **Height:** 6–4; **Weight:** 215; **NFL Years:** 5

		RECEIVING				
Year	Club	No.	Yds.	Avg.	Lg.	TDs
1981	Miami	0	0	0.0	0	0
1982	Miami	0	0	0.0	0	0
1983	Miami	0	0	0.0	0	0
1984	Miami	13	139	10.7	20	2
1985	Miami	1	4	4.0	4t	1
Totals		**14**	**143**	**10.2**	**20**	**3**

JOHNSON, Billy 'White Shoes' ATLANTA FALCONS
Position: Wide Receiver; **Birthdate:** 27.01.52
College: Widener; **Height:** 5–9; **Weight:** 170; **NFL Years:** 10

		RECEIVING				
Year	Club	No.	Yds.	Avg.	Lg.	TDs
1974	Houston	29	388	13.4	44	2
1975	Houston	37	393	10.6	30	1
1976	Houston	47	495	10.5	40t	4
1977	Houston	20	412	20.6	71t	3
1978	Houston	1	10	10.0	10	0
1979	Houston	6	108	18.0	29	1
1980	Houston	31	343	11.1	57t	2
1981				Did not play		
1982	Atlanta	2	11	5.5	6	0
1983	Atlanta	64	709	11.1	47t	4
1984	Atlanta	24	371	15.5	45t	3
1985	Atlanta	62	830	13.4	62t	5
Totals		**323**	**4,070**	**12.6**	**71t**	**25**

JOHNSON, Bill CINCINNATI BENGALS
Position: Running Back; **Birthdate:** 31.10.60
College: Arkansas State; **Height:** 6–2; **Weight:** 230; **NFL Years:** 1

		RUSHING					RECEIVING			
Year	Club	Att.	Yds.	Avg.	Lg.	TDs	No.	Yds.	Avg.	Lg.	TDs
1985	Cincinnati	8	44	5.5	15	0	0	0	0.0	0	0
Totals		**8**	**44**	**5.5**	**15**	**0**	**0**	**0**	**0.0**	**0**	**0**

JOHNSON, Bob NEW YORK GIANTS
Position: Wide Receiver; **Birthdate:** 14.12.61
College: Kansas; **Height:** 5–11; **Weight:** 171; **NFL Years:** 2

		RECEIVING			
Year	Club	No.	Yds.	Avg.	Lg.	TDs
1984	N.Y. Giants	48	795	16.6	45	7
1985	N.Y. Giants	33	533	16.2	42	8
Totals		**81**	**1,328**	**16.4**	**45**	**15**

BILLY JOHNSON

BOB JOHNSON

JOHNSON, Butch DENVER BRONCOS
Position: Wide Receiver; **Birthdate:** 28.05.54
College: California-Riverside; **Height:** 6–1; **Weight:** 187; **NFL Years:** 10

		RECEIVING				
Year	Club	No.	Yds.	Avg.	Lg.	TDs
1976	Dallas	5	84	16.8	43t	2
1977	Dallas	12	135	11.3	22t	1
1978	Dallas	12	155	12.9	23	0
1979	Dallas	6	105	17.5	28	1
1980	Dallas	19	263	13.8	29t	4
1981	Dallas	25	552	22.1	55	5
1982	Dallas	12	269	22.4	49	3
1983	Dallas	41	561	13.7	46	3
1984	Denver	42	587	14.0	49	6
1985	Denver	19	380	20.0	65t	3
Totals		**193**	**3,091**	**16.0**	**65t**	**28**

JOHNSON, Dan MIAMI DOLPHINS
Position: Tight End; **Birthdate:** 17.05.60
College: Iowa State; **Height:** 6–3; **Weight:** 240; **NFL Years:** 3

		RECEIVING				
Year	Club	No.	Yds.	Avg.	Lg.	TDs
1982	Miami		Did not play			
1983	Miami	24	189	7.9	33	4
1984	Miami	34	426	12.5	42	3
1985	Miami	13	192	14.8	61t	3
Totals		**71**	**807**	**11.4**	**61t**	**10**

JOHNSON, Norm SEATTLE SEAHAWKS
Position: Placekicker; **Birthdate:** 31.05.60
College: UCLA; **Height:** 6–2; **Weight:** 193; **NFL Years:** 4

		SCORING					
Year	Club	EPA	EPM	FGA	FGM	Lg.	Pts.
1982	Seattle	14	13	14	10	48	43
1983	Seattle	50	49	25	18	54	103

BUTCH JOHNSON

DAN JOHNSON

Year	Club	EPA	EPM	FGA	FGM	Lg.	Pts.
1984	Seattle	51	50	24	20	50	110
1985	Seattle	41	40	25	14	51	82
Totals		**156**	**152**	**88**	**62**	**54**	**338**

JOHNSON, Trumaine SAN DIEGO CHARGERS
Position: Wide Receiver; **Birthdate:** 16.01.60
College: Grambling State; **Height:** 6–3; **Weight:** 196; **NFL Years:** 1

		RECEIVING				
Year	Club	No.	Yds.	Avg.	Lg.	TDs
1985	San Diego	4	51	12.8	20t	1
Totals		**4**	**51**	**12.8**	**20t**	**1**

JOHNSON, Vance DENVER BRONCOS
Position: Wide Receiver; **Birthdate:** 13.03.63
College: Arizona; **Height:** 5–11; **Weight:** 174; **NFL Years:** 1

		RECEIVING				
Year	Club	No.	Yds.	Avg.	Lg.	TDs
1985	Denver	51	721	14.1	63t	3
Totals		**51**	**721**	**14.1**	**63t**	**3**

JOINER, Charlie SAN DIEGO CHARGERS
Position: Wide Receiver; **Birthdate:** 14.10.47
College: Grambling State; **Height:** 5–11; **Weight:** 177; **NFL Years:** 17

| | | **RECEIVING** | | | | |
Year	Club	No.	Yds.	Avg.	Lg.	TDs
1969	Houston	7	77	11.0	21	0
1970	Houston	28	416	14.9	87t	3
1971	Houston	31	681	22.0	55	7
1972	Hou.–Cin.	24	439	18.3	82t	2
1973	Cincinnati	13	214	16.5	26	0
1974	Cincinnati	24	390	16.3	55	1
1975	Cincinnati	37	726	19.6	51	5
1976	San Diego	50	1,056	21.1	81t	7
1977	San Diego	35	542	15.5	32t	6
1978	San Diego	33	607	18.4	46	1
1979	San Diego	72	1,008	14.0	39	4
1980	San Diego	71	1,132	15.9	51	4
1981	San Diego	70	1,188	17.0	57	7
1982	San Diego	36	545	15.1	43	0
1983	San Diego	65	960	14.8	33t	3
1984	San Diego	61	793	13.0	41	6
1985	San Diego	59	932	15.8	39t	7
Totals		**716**	**11,706**	**16.3**	**87t**	**63**

CHARLIE JOINER

CEDRIC JONES

JONES, Anthony WASHINGTON REDSKINS
Position: Tight End; **Birthdate:** 16.05.60
College: Wichita State; **Height:** 6–3; **Weight:** 248; **NFL Years:** 2

		RECEIVING				
Year	Club	No.	Yds.	Avg.	Lg.	TDs
1984	Washington	1	6	6.0	6	0
1985	Washington	0	0	0.0	0	0
Totals		**1**	**6**	**6.0**	**6**	**0**

JONES, Cedric NEW ENGLAND PATRIOTS
Position: Wide Receiver; **Birthdate:** 01.06.60
College: Duke; **Height:** 6–1; **Weight:** 184; **NFL Years:** 4

		RECEIVING				
Year	Club	No.	Yds.	Avg.	Lg.	TDs
1982	New England	1	5	5.0	5	0
1983	New England	20	323	16.2	30	1
1984	New England	19	244	12.8	22	2
1985	New England	21	237	11.3	29t	2
Totals		**61**	**809**	**13.3**	**30**	**5**

JONES, James DALLAS COWBOYS
Position: Running Back; **Birthdate:** 06.12.58
College: Mississippi State; **Height:** 5–10; **Weight:** 203; **NFL Years:** 5

		RUSHING					RECEIVING				
Year	Club	Att.	Yds.	Avg.	Lg.	TDs	No.	Yds.	Avg.	Lg.	TDs
1980	Dallas	41	135	3.3	9	0	5	39	7.8	16	0
1981	Dallas	34	183	5.4	59t	1	6	37	6.2	16	0
1982	Dallas	0	0	0.0	0	0	0	0	0.0	0	0
1983	Dallas					Did not play					
1984	Dallas	8	13	1.6	6	0	7	57	8.1	19	1
1985	Dallas	1	0	0.0	0	0	24	179	7.5	35	0
Totals		**84**	**331**	**3.9**	**59t**	**1**	**42**	**312**	**7.4**	**35**	**1**

JONES, James DETROIT LIONS
Position: Running Back; **Birthdate:** 21.03.61
College: Florida; **Height:** 6–2; **Weight:** 229; **NFL Years:** 3

		RUSHING					RECEIVING				
Year	Club	Att.	Yds.	Avg.	Lg.	TDs	No.	Yds.	Avg.	Lg.	TDs
1983	Detroit	135	475	3.5	18	6	46	467	10.2	46	1
1984	Detroit	137	532	3.9	34	3	77	662	8.6	39	5
1985	Detroit	244	886	3.6	29	6	45	334	7.4	36	3
Totals		**516**	**1,893**	**3.7**	**34**	**15**	**168**	**1,463**	**8.7**	**46**	**9**

JONES, Johnny 'Lam' NEW YORK JETS
Position: Wide Receiver; **Birthdate:** 04.04.58
College: Texas; **Height:** 5–11; **Weight:** 180; **NFL Years:** 5

		RECEIVING			
Year	Club	No.	Yds.	Avg.	Lg.	TDs
1980	N.Y. Jets	25	482	19.3	55	3
1981	N.Y. Jets	20	342	17.1	47t	3
1982	N.Y. Jets	18	294	16.3	51	2
1983	N.Y. Jets	43	734	17.1	50t	4
1984	N.Y. Jets	32	470	14.7	37	1
1985	N.Y. Jets			Did not play		
Totals		**138**	**2,322**	**16.8**	**55**	**13**

JONES, Mike MINNESOTA VIKINGS
Position: Wide Receiver; **Birthdate:** 14.04.60
College: Tennessee State; **Height:** 5–11; **Weight:** 180; **NFL Years:** 3

		RECEIVING			
Year	Club	No.	Yds.	Avg.	Lg.	TDs
1983	Minnesota	6	95	15.8	47	0
1984	Minnesota	38	591	15.6	70t	1
1985	Minnesota	46	641	13.9	44t	4
Totals		**90**	**1,327**	**14.7**	**70t**	**5**

JORDAN, Steve MINNESOTA VIKINGS
Position: Tight End; **Birthdate:** 10.01.61
College: Brown; **Height:** 6–3; **Weight:** 231; **NFL Years:** 4

		RECEIVING				
Year	Club	No.	Yds.	Avg.	Lg.	TDs
1982	Minnesota	3	42	14.0	29	0
1983	Minnesota	15	212	14.1	28	2
1984	Minnesota	38	414	10.9	26	2
1985	Minnesota	68	795	11.7	32	0
Totals		**124**	**1,463**	**11.8**	**32**	**4**

KAB, Vyto NEW YORK GIANTS
Position: Tight End; **Birthdate:** 23.12.59
College: Penn State; **Height:** 6–5; **Weight:** 240; **NFL Years:** 4

		RECEIVING				
Year	Club	No.	Yds.	Avg.	Lg.	TDs
1982	Philadelphia	4	35	8.8	13	1
1983	Philadelphia	18	195	10.8	25	1
1984	Philadelphia	9	102	11.3	26	3
1985	N.Y. Giants	0	0	0.0	0	0
Totals		**31**	**332**	**10.7**	**26**	**5**

JAMES JONES (DETROIT)

STEVE JORDAN

RICH KARLIS

BILL KENNEY

KARLIS, Rich DENVER BRONCOS
Position: Placekicker; **Birthdate:** 23.05.59
College: Cincinnati; **Height:** 6–0; **Weight:** 180; **NFL Years:** 4

				SCORING			
Year	Club	EPA	EPM	FGA	FGM	Lg.	Pts.
1982	Denver	16	15	13	11	47	48
1983	Denver	34	33	25	21	50	96
1984	Denver	41	38	28	21	50	101
1985	Denver	44	41	38	23	48	110
Totals		**135**	**127**	**104**	**76**	**50**	**355**

KAY, Clarence DENVER BRONCOS
Position: Tight End; **Birthdate:** 30.07.61
College: Georgia; **Height:** 6–2; **Weight:** 237; **NFL Years:** 2

			RECEIVING			
Year	Club	No.	Yds.	Avg.	Lg.	TDs
1984	Denver	16	136	8.5	21	3
1985	Denver	29	339	11.7	27	3
Totals		**45**	**475**	**10.6**	**27**	**6**

KEMP, Jeff SAN FRANCISCO 49ers
Position: Quarterback; **Birthdate:** 11.07.59
College: Dartmouth; **Height:** 6–1; **Weight:** 201; **NFL Years:** 5

		PASSING						
Year	**Club**	**Att.**	**Comp.**	**Yds.**	**Lg.**	**TDs**	**Int.**	**Rat.**
1981	L.A. Rams	6	2	25	19	0	1	7.6
1982	L.A. Rams	0	0	0	0	0	0	00.0
1983	L.A. Rams	25	12	135	21	1	0	77.9
1984	L.A. Rams	284	143	2,021	63t	13	7	78.7
1985	L.A. Rams	38	16	214	35	0	1	49.7
Totals		**353**	**173**	**2,395**	**63t**	**14**	**9**	**73.8**

KENNEY, Bill KANSAS CITY CHIEFS
Position: Quarterback; **Birthdate:** 20.01.55
College: Northern Colorado; **Height:** 6–4; **Weight:** 211; **NFL Years:** 7

		PASSING						
Year	**Club**	**Att.**	**Comp.**	**Yds.**	**Lg.**	**TDs**	**Int.**	**Rat.**
1979	Kansas City	0	0	0	0	0	0	00.0
1980	Kansas City	69	37	542	75t	5	2	91.4
1981	Kansas City	274	147	1,983	64t	9	16	63.8
1982	Kansas City	169	95	1,192	51	7	6	77.0
1983	Kansas City	603	346	4,348	53	24	18	80.8
1984	Kansas City	282	151	2,098	65t	15	10	80.7
1985	Kansas City	338	181	2,536	84t	17	9	83.6
Totals		**1,735**	**957**	**12,699**	**84t**	**77**	**61**	**78.7**

KERN, Don CINCINNATI BENGALS
Position: Tight End; **Birthdate:** 25.08.62
College: Arizona State; **Height:** 6–4; **Weight:** 225; **NFL Years:** 2

		RECEIVING			
Year	**Club**	**No.**	**Yds.**	**Avg.**	**Lg.**	**TDs**
1984	Cincinnati	2	14	7.0	9	0
1985	Cincinnati	0	0	0.0	0	0
Totals		**2**	**14**	**7.0**	**9**	**0**

113

KING, Bruce KANSAS CITY CHIEFS
Position: Running Back; **Birthdate:** 07.01.63
College: Purdue; **Height:** 6–1; **Weight:** 219; **NFL Years:** 1

Year	Club	RUSHING					RECEIVING				
		Att.	Yds.	Avg.	Lg.	TDs	No.	Yds.	Avg.	Lg.	TDs
1985	Kansas City	28	83	3.0	9	0	7	45	6.4	8	0
Totals		**28**	**83**	**3.0**	**9**	**0**	**7**	**45**	**6.4**	**8**	**0**

KING, Kenny LOS ANGELES RAIDERS
Position: Running Back; **Birthdate:** 07.03.57
College: Oklahoma; **Height:** 5–11; **Weight:** 205; **NFL Years:** 7

Year	Club	RUSHING					RECEIVING				
		Att.	Yds.	Avg.	Lg.	TDs	No.	Yds.	Avg.	Lg.	TDs
1979	Houston	3	9	3.0	4	0	0	0	0.0	0	0
1980	Oakland	172	761	4.4	89t	4	22	145	6.6	18	0
1981	Oakland	170	828	4.9	60	0	27	216	8.0	30	0
1982	L.A. Raiders	69	264	3.8	21	2	9	57	6.3	20	0
1983	L.A. Raiders	82	294	3.6	16	1	14	149	10.6	34t	1
1984	L.A. Raiders	67	254	3.8	18	0	14	99	7.1	15	0
1985	L.A. Raiders	16	67	4.2	19	0	3	49	16.3	37	0
Totals		**579**	**2,477**	**4.3**	**89t**	**7**	**89**	**715**	**8.0**	**37**	**1**

KENNY KING

LARRY KINNEBREW

KINNEBREW, Larry CINCINNATI BENGALS
Position: Running Back; **Birthdate:** 11.06.59
College: Tennessee State; **Height:** 6–1; **Weight:** 252; **NFL Years:** 3

		RUSHING					RECEIVING				
Year	Club	Att.	Yds.	Avg.	Lg.	TDs	No.	Yds.	Avg.	Lg.	TDs
1983	Cincinnati	39	156	4.0	17	3	2	4	2.0	2	0
1984	Cincinnati	154	623	4.0	23	9	19	159	8.4	22	1
1985	Cincinnati	170	714	4.2	29	9	22	187	8.5	29t	1
Totals		**363**	**1,493**	**4.1**	**29**	**21**	**43**	**350**	**8.1**	**29t**	**2**

KLEVER, Rocky NEW YORK JETS
Position: Tight End; **Birthdate:** 10.07.59
College: Montana; **Height:** 6–3; **Weight:** 225; **NFL Years:** 3

		RECEIVING			
Year	Club	No.	Yds.	Avg.	Lg.	TDs
1982	N.Y. Jets			Did not play		
1983	N.Y. Jets	0	0	0.0	0	0
1984	N.Y. Jets	3	29	9.7	13	1
1985	N.Y. Jets	14	183	13.1	23	2
Totals		**17**	**212**	**12.5**	**23**	**3**

KOFLER, Matt INDIANAPOLIS COLTS
Position: Quarterback; **Birthdate:** 30.08.59
College: San Diego State; **Height:** 6–3; **Weight:** 192; **NFL Years:** 4

		PASSING						
Year	Club	Att.	Comp.	Yds.	Lg.	TDs	Int.	Rat.
1982	Buffalo	0	0	0	0	0	0	00.0
1983	Buffalo	61	35	440	28t	4	3	81.3
1984	Buffalo	93	33	432	70t	2	5	35.8
1985	Indianapolis	48	23	284	33t	1	3	47.6
Totals		**202**	**91**	**1,156**	**70t**	**7**	**11**	**52.3**

KOSAR, Bernie CLEVELAND BROWNS
Position: Quarterback; **Birthdate:** 25.11.63
College: Miami; **Height:** 6–5; **Weight:** 210; **NFL Years:** 1

		PASSING						
Year	**Club**	**Att.**	**Comp.**	**Yds.**	**Lg.**	**TDs**	**Int.**	**Rat.**
1985	Cleveland	248	124	1,578	68t	8	7	69.3
Totals		**248**	**124**	**1,578**	**68t**	**8**	**7**	**69.3**

KRAMER, Tommy MINNESOTA VIKINGS
Position: Quarterback; **Birthdate:** 07.03.55
College: Rice; **Height:** 6–2; **Weight:** 202; **NFL Years:** 9

		PASSING						
Year	**Club**	**Att.**	**Comp.**	**Yds.**	**Lg.**	**TDs**	**Int.**	**Rat.**
1977	Minnesota	57	30	425	69t	5	4	77.2
1978	Minnesota	16	5	50	19	0	1	15.0
1979	Minnesota	566	315	3,397	55t	23	24	69.7
1980	Minnesota	522	299	3,582	76t	19	23	72.1
1981	Minnesota	593	322	3,912	63	26	24	72.8
1982	Minnesota	308	176	2,037	65	15	12	77.3
1983	Minnesota	82	55	550	49	3	4	77.8
1984	Minnesota	236	124	1,678	70t	9	10	70.6
1985	Minnesota	506	277	3,522	57t	19	26	67.8
Totals		**2,886**	**1,603**	**19,153**	**76t**	**119**	**128**	**71.3**

KREIDER, Steve CINCINNATI BENGALS
Position: Wide Receiver; **Birthdate:** 12.05.58
College: Lehigh; **Height:** 6–3; **Weight:** 192; **NFL Years:** 7

		RECEIVING				
Year	**Club**	**No.**	**Yds.**	**Avg.**	**Lg.**	**TDs**
1979	Cincinnati	3	20	6.7	8	0
1980	Cincinnati	17	272	16.0	30	0
1981	Cincinnati	37	520	14.1	46	5
1982	Cincinnati	16	230	14.4	28	1

Year	Club	No.	Yds.	Avg.	Lg.	TDs
1983	Cincinnati	42	554	13.2	54	1
1984	Cincinnati	20	243	12.2	27	1
1985	Cincinnati	10	184	18.4	56	1
Totals		**145**	**2,023**	**14.0**	**56**	**9**

KRIEG, Dave SEATTLE SEAHAWKS
Position: Quarterback; **Birthdate:** 20.10.58
College: Milton; **Height:** 6–1; **Weight:** 185; **NFL Years:** 6

				PASSING				
Year	Club	Att.	Comp.	Yds.	Lg.	TDs	Int.	Rat.
1980	Seattle	2	0	0	0	0	0	00.0
1981	Seattle	112	64	843	57t	7	5	83.3
1982	Seattle	78	49	501	44	2	2	79.0
1983	Seattle	243	147	2,139	50t	18	11	95.0
1984	Seattle	480	276	3,671	80t	32	24	83.3
1985	Seattle	532	285	3,602	54	27	20	76.2
Totals		**1,447**	**821**	**10,756**	**80t**	**86**	**62**	**82.3**

BERNIE KOSAR

DAVE KRIEG

117

KUBIAK, Gary DENVER BRONCOS
Position: Quarterback; **Birthdate:** 15.08.61
College: Texas A&M; **Height:** 6–0; **Weight:** 192; **NFL Years:** 3

		PASSING						
Year	**Club**	**Att.**	**Comp.**	**Yds.**	**Lg.**	**TDs**	**Int.**	**Rat.**
1983	Denver	22	12	186	78t	1	1	79.0
1984	Denver	75	44	440	41	4	1	87.6
1985	Denver	5	2	61	54t	1	0	125.8
Totals		**102**	**58**	**687**	**78t**	**6**	**2**	**89.0**

LaFLEUR, Greg ST. LOUIS CARDINALS
Position: Tight End; **Birthdate:** 16.09.58
College: LSU; **Height:** 6–4; **Weight:** 236; **NFL Years:** 5

		RECEIVING				
Year	**Club**	**No.**	**Yds.**	**Avg.**	**Lg.**	**TDs**
1981	St. Louis	14	190	13.6	27t	2
1982	St. Louis	5	67	13.4	20	1
1983	St. Louis	12	99	8.3	21	0
1984	St. Louis	17	198	11.6	23	0
1985	St. Louis	9	119	13.2	24	0
Totals		**57**	**673**	**11.8**	**27t**	**3**

LANDRUM, Mike ATLANTA FALCONS
Position: Tight End; **Birthdate:** 06.11.61
College: Southern Mississippi; **Height:** 6–2; **Weight:** 231; **NFL Years:** 1

		RECEIVING				
Year	**Club**	**No.**	**Yds.**	**Avg.**	**Lg.**	**TDs**
1984	Atlanta	6	66	11.0	30	0
1985	Atlanta			Did not play		
Totals		**6**	**66**	**11.0**	**30**	**0**

GARY KUBIAK

GENE LANG

LANE, Eric SEATTLE SEAHAWKS
Position: Running Back; **Birthdate:** 06.01.59
College: Brigham Young; **Height:** 6–0; **Weight:** 195; **NFL Years:** 5

Year	Club	Att.	Yds.	Avg.	Lg.	TDs	No.	Yds.	Avg.	Lg.	TDs
			RUSHING					**RECEIVING**			
1981	Seattle	8	22	2.8	5	0	7	58	8.3	22	0
1982	Seattle	0	0	0.0	0	0	0	0	0.0	0	0
1983	Seattle	3	1	0.3	7	0	2	9	4.5	7	0
1984	Seattle	80	299	3.7	40t	4	11	101	9.2	55t	1
1985	Seattle	14	32	2.3	12	0	15	153	10.2	20	0
Totals		**105**	**354**	**3.4**	**40t**	**4**	**35**	**321**	**9.2**	**55t**	**1**

LANG, Gene DENVER BRONCOS
Position: Running Back; **Birthdate:** 15.03.62
College: Louisiana State; **Height:** 5–10; **Weight:** 196; **NFL Years:** 2

Year	Club	Att.	Yds.	Avg.	Lg.	TDs	No.	Yds.	Avg.	Lg.	TDs
			RUSHING					**RECEIVING**			
1984	Denver	8	42	5.3	15	2	4	24	6.0	9t	1
1985	Denver	84	318	3.8	26	5	23	180	7.8	24	2
Totals		**92**	**360**	**3.9**	**26**	**7**	**27**	**204**	**7.6**	**24**	**3**

LANSFORD, Mike LOS ANGELES RAMS
Position: Placekicker; **Birthdate:** 20.07.58
College: Washington; **Height:** 6–0; **Weight:** 183; **NFL Years:** 4

		SCORING					
Year	Club	EPA	EPM	FGA	FGM	Lg.	Pts.
1982	L.A. Rams	24	23	15	9	39	50
1983	L.A. Rams	9	9	9	6	49	27
1984	L.A. Rams	38	37	33	25	50	112
1985	L.A. Rams	39	38	29	22	52	104
Totals		**110**	**107**	**86**	**62**	**52**	**293**

LARGENT, Steve SEATTLE SEAHAWKS
Position: Wide Receiver; **Birthdate:** 28.09.54
College: Tulsa; **Height:** 5–11; **Weight:** 184; **NFL Years:** 10

		RECEIVING				
Year	Club	No.	Yds.	Avg.	Lg.	TDs
1976	Seattle	54	705	13.1	45	4
1977	Seattle	33	643	19.5	74t	10
1978	Seattle	71	1,168	16.5	57t	8
1979	Seattle	66	1,237	18.7	55t	9
1980	Seattle	66	1,064	16.1	67t	6
1981	Seattle	75	1,224	16.3	57t	9
1982	Seattle	34	493	14.5	45	3
1983	Seattle	72	1,074	14.9	46t	11
1984	Seattle	74	1,164	15.7	65	12
1985	Seattle	79	1,287	16.3	43	6
Totals		**624**	**10,059**	**16.1**	**74t**	**78**

LEAHY, Pat NEW YORK JETS
Position: Placekicker; **Birthdate:** 19.03.51
College: St. Louis; **Height:** 6–0; **Weight:** 193; **NFL Years:** 12

		SCORING					
Year	Club	EPA	EPM	FGA	FGM	Lg.	Pts.
1974	N.Y. Jets	19	18	11	6	45	36
1975	N.Y. Jets	30	27	21	13	47	66

Year	Club	EPA	EPM	FGA	FGM	Lg.	Pts.
1976	N.Y. Jets	20	16	16	11	47	49
1977	N.Y. Jets	21	18	25	15	48	63
1978	N.Y. Jets	42	41	30	22	47	107
1979	N.Y. Jets	15	12	13	8	34	36
1980	N.Y. Jets	36	36	22	14	49	78
1981	N.Y. Jets	39	38	36	25	49	113
1982	N.Y. Jets	31	26	17	11	49	59
1983	N.Y. Jets	37	36	24	16	49	84
1984	N.Y. Jets	39	38	24	17	52	89
1985	N.Y. Jets	45	43	34	26	55	121
Totals		**374**	**349**	**273**	**171**	**55**	**901**

LEWIS, David DETROIT LIONS
Position: Tight End; **Birthdate:** 08.06.61
College: California; **Height:** 6–3; **Weight:** 235; **NFL Years:** 2

		RECEIVING			
Year	Club	No.	Yds.	Avg.	Lg.	TDs
1984	Detroit	16	236	14.8	58	3
1985	Detroit	28	354	12.6	40	3
Totals		**44**	**590**	**13.4**	**58**	**6**

MIKE LANSFORD

STEVE LARGENT

121

LOUIS LIPPS

JAMES LOFTON

LEWIS, Leo MINNESOTA VIKINGS
Position: Wide Receiver; **Birthdate:** 17.09.56
College: Missouri; **Height:** 5–8; **Weight:** 172; **NFL Years:** 5

		RECEIVING				
Year	Club	No.	Yds.	Avg.	Lg.	TDs
1979	St. Louis			Did not play		
1980				Did not play		
1981	Minnesota	2	58	29.0	52	0
1982	Minnesota	8	150	18.8	39t	3
1983	Minnesota	12	127	10.6	18	0
1984	Minnesota	47	830	17.7	56	4
1985	Minnesota	29	442	15.2	43t	3
Totals		**98**	**1,607**	**16.4**	**56**	**10**

LEWIS, Mark GREEN BAY PACKERS
Position: Tight End; **Birthdate:** 20.05.61
College: Texas A&M; **Height:** 6–2; **Weight:** 218; **NFL Years:** 1

		RECEIVING				
Year	Club	No.	Yds.	Avg.	Lg.	TDs
1985	Green Bay	0	0	0.0	0	0
Totals		**0**	**0**	**0.0**	**0**	**0**

122

LIPPS, Louis PITTSBURGH STEELERS
Position: Wide Receiver; **Birthdate:** 09.08.62
College: Southern Mississippi; **Height:** 5–10; **Weight:** 186; **NFL Years:** 2

		RECEIVING				
Year	Club	No.	Yds.	Avg.	Lg.	TDs
1984	Pittsburgh	45	860	19.1	80t	9
1985	Pittsburgh	59	1,134	19.2	51	12
Totals		**104**	**1,994**	**19.2**	**80t**	**21**

LOFTON, James GREEN BAY PACKERS
Position: Wide Receiver; **Birthdate:** 05.07.56
College: Stanford; **Height:** 6–3; **Weight:** 197; **NFL Years:** 8

		RECEIVING				
Year	Club	No.	Yds.	Avg.	Lg.	TDs
1978	Green Bay	46	818	17.8	58t	6
1979	Green Bay	54	968	17.9	52	4
1980	Green Bay	71	1,226	17.3	47	4
1981	Green Bay	71	1,294	18.2	75t	8
1982	Green Bay	35	696	19.9	80t	4
1983	Green Bay	58	1,300	22.4	74t	8
1984	Green Bay	62	1,361	22.0	79t	7
1985	Green Bay	69	1,153	16.7	56t	4
Totals		**466**	**8,816**	**18.9**	**80t**	**45**

LOMAX, Neil ST. LOUIS CARDINALS
Position: Quarterback; **Birthdate:** 17.02.59
College: Portland State; **Height:** 6–3; **Weight:** 215; **NFL Years:** 5

		PASSING						
Year	Club	Att.	Comp.	Yds.	Lg.	TDs	Int.	Rat.
1981	St. Louis	236	119	1,575	75	4	10	60.1
1982	St. Louis	205	109	1,367	42	5	6	70.1
1983	St. Louis	354	209	2,636	71t	24	11	92.0
1984	St. Louis	560	345	4,614	83t	28	16	92.5
1985	St. Louis	471	265	3,214	47	18	12	79.5
Totals		**1,826**	**1,047**	**13,406**	**83t**	**79**	**55**	**82.3**

LOWERY, Nick KANSAS CITY CHIEFS
Position: Placekicker; **Birthdate:** 27.05.56
College: Dartmouth; **Height:** 6–4; **Weight:** 189; **NFL Years:** 6

		SCORING					
Year	Club	EPA	EPM	FGA	FGM	Lg.	Pts.
1978	New England	7	7	1	0	00	7
1979		Did not play					
1980	Kansas City	37	37	26	20	57	97
1981	Kansas City	38	37	36	26	52	115
1982	Kansas City	17	17	24	19	47	74
1983	Kansas City	45	44	30	24	58	116
1984	Kansas City	35	35	33	23	52	104
1985	Kansas City	35	35	27	24	58	107
Totals		**214**	**212**	**177**	**136**	**58**	**620**

LUCK, Oliver HOUSTON OILERS
Position: Quarterback; **Birthdate:** 05.04.60
College: West Virginia; **Height:** 6–2; **Weight:** 196; **NFL Years:** 4

		PASSING						
Year	Club	Att.	Comp.	Yds.	Lg.	TDs	Int.	Rat.
1982	Houston	0	0	0	0	0	0	00.0
1983	Houston	217	124	1,375	66	8	13	63.4

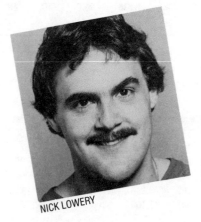

NICK LOWERY

MARK MALONE

Year	Club	Att.	Comp.	Yds.	Lg.	TDs	Int.	Rat.
1984	Houston	36	22	256	37	2	1	89.6
1985	Houston	100	56	572	46t	2	2	70.9
Totals		**353**	**202**	**2,203**	**66**	**12**	**16**	**68.2**

LUCKHURST, Mick ATLANTA FALCONS
Position: Placekicker; **Birthdate:** 31.03.58
College: California; **Height:** 6–2; **Weight:** 183; **NFL Years:** 5

				SCORING			
Year	Club	EPA	EPM	FGA	FGM	Lg.	Pts.
1981	Atlanta	51	51	33	21	47	114
1982	Atlanta	22	21	14	10	51	51
1983	Atlanta	45	43	22	17	49	94
1984	Atlanta	31	31	27	20	52	91
1985	Atlanta	29	29	31	24	52	101
Totals		**178**	**175**	**127**	**92**	**52**	**451**

MACK, Kevin CLEVELAND BROWNS
Position: Running Back; **Birthdate:** 09.08.62
College: Clemson; **Height:** 6–0; **Weight:** 212; **NFL Years:** 1

		RUSHING					RECEIVING				
Year	Club	Att.	Yds.	Avg.	Lg.	TDs	No.	Yds.	Avg.	Lg.	TDs
1985	Cleveland	222	1,104	5.0	61	7	29	297	10.2	43	3
Totals		**222**	**1,104**	**5.0**	**61**	**7**	**29**	**297**	**10.2**	**43**	**3**

MALONE, Mark PITTSBURGH STEELERS
Position: Quarterback; **Birthdate:** 22.11.58
College: Arizona State; **Height:** 6–4; **Weight:** 222; **NFL Years:** 6

				PASSING				
Year	Club	Att.	Comp.	Yds.	Lg.	TDs	Int.	Rat.
1980	Pittsburgh	0	0	0	0	0	0	00.0
1981	Pittsburgh	88	45	553	30	3	5	58.4
1982	Pittsburgh	0	0	0	0	0	0	00.0
1983	Pittsburgh	20	9	124	38	1	2	42.5
1984	Pittsburgh	272	147	2,137	61t	16	17	73.4
1985	Pittsburgh	233	117	1,428	45t	13	7	75.5
Totals		**613**	**318**	**4,242**	**61t**	**33**	**31**	**71.0**

LIONEL MANUEL

DOUG MARSH

MANDLEY, Pete DETROIT LIONS
Position: Wide Receiver; **Birthdate:** 29.07.61
College: Northern Arizona; **Height:** 5–10; **Weight:** 191; **NFL Years:** 2

		RECEIVING				
Year	Club	No.	Yds.	Avg.	Lg.	TDs
1984	Detroit	3	38	12.7	19	0
1985	Detroit	18	316	17.6	37	0
Totals		**21**	**354**	**16.9**	**37**	**0**

MANUEL, Lionel NEW YORK GIANTS
Position: Wide Receiver; **Birthdate:** 13.04.62
College: Pacific; **Height:** 5–11; **Weight:** 175; **NFL Years:** 2

		RECEIVING				
Year	Club	No.	Yds.	Avg.	Lg.	TDs
1984	N.Y. Giants	33	619	18.8	53	4
1985	N.Y. Giants	49	859	17.5	51t	5
Totals		**82**	**1,478**	**18.0**	**53**	**9**

MARGERUM, Ken CHICAGO BEARS
Position: Wide Receiver; **Birthdate:** 05.10.58
College: Stanford; **Height:** 6–0; **Weight:** 180; **NFL Years:** 4

		RECEIVING				
Year	Club	No.	Yds.	Avg.	Lg.	TDs
1981	Chicago	39	584	15.0	41	1
1982	Chicago	14	207	14.8	28	3
1983	Chicago	21	336	16.0	60	2
1984	Chicago			Did not play		
1985	Chicago	17	190	11.2	20	2
Totals		**91**	**1,317**	**14.5**	**60**	**8**

MARINO, Dan MIAMI DOLPHINS
Position: Quarterback; **Birthdate:** 15.09.61
College: Pittsburgh; **Height:** 6–4; **Weight:** 214; **NFL Years:** 3

		PASSING						
Year	Club	Att.	Comp.	Yds.	Lg.	TDs	Int.	Rat.
1983	Miami	296	173	2,210	85t	20	6	96.0
1984	Miami	564	362	5,084	80t	48	17	108.9
1985	Miami	567	336	4,137	73	30	21	84.1
Totals		**1,427**	**871**	**11,431**	**85t**	**98**	**44**	**96.4**

MARSH, Doug ST. LOUIS CARDINALS
Position: Tight End; **Birthdate:** 18.06.58
College: Michigan; **Height:** 6–3; **Weight:** 238; **NFL Years:** 6

		RECEIVING				
Year	Club	No.	Yds.	Avg.	Lg.	TDs
1980	St. Louis	22	269	12.2	29	4
1981	St. Louis	6	80	13.3	20	1
1982	St. Louis	5	83	16.6	21	0
1983	St. Louis	32	421	13.2	38	8
1984	St. Louis	39	608	15.6	47	5
1985	St. Louis	37	355	9.6	23	1
Totals		**141**	**1,816**	**12.9**	**47**	**19**

MARSHALL, Henry KANSAS CITY CHIEFS
Position: Wide Receiver; **Birthdate:** 09.08.54
College: Missouri; **Height:** 6–2; **Weight:** 213; **NFL Years:** 10

		RECEIVING				
Year	**Club**	**No.**	**Yds.**	**Avg.**	**Lg.**	**TDs**
1976	Kansas City	28	443	15.8	31t	2
1977	Kansas City	23	445	19.3	49	4
1978	Kansas City	26	433	16.7	40	2
1979	Kansas City	21	332	15.8	38t	1
1980	Kansas City	47	799	17.0	75t	6
1981	Kansas City	38	620	16.3	64t	4
1982	Kansas City	40	549	13.7	44t	3
1983	Kansas City	50	788	15.8	52	6
1984	Kansas City	62	912	14.7	37	4
1985	Kansas City	25	446	17.8	50	0
Totals		**360**	**5,767**	**16.0**	**75t**	**32**

MARTIN, Eric NEW ORLEANS SAINTS
Position: Wide Receiver; **Birthdate:** 08.11.61
College: Louisiana State; **Height:** 6–1; **Weight:** 195; **NFL Years:** 1

		RECEIVING				
Year	**Club**	**No.**	**Yds.**	**Avg.**	**Lg.**	**TDs**
1985	New Orleans	35	522	14.9	50	4
Totals		**35**	**522**	**14.9**	**50**	**4**

MARTIN, Mike CINCINNATI BENGALS
Position: Wide Receiver; **Birthdate:** 18.11.60
College: Illinois; **Height:** 5–10; **Weight:** 186; **NFL Years:** 3

		RECEIVING				
Year	**Club**	**No.**	**Yds.**	**Avg.**	**Lg.**	**TDs**
1983	Cincinnati	2	22	11.0	12	0
1984	Cincinnati	11	164	14.9	42	0
1985	Cincinnati	14	187	13.4	28	0
Totals		**27**	**373**	**13.8**	**42**	**0**

MARTIN, Robbie INDIANAPOLIS COLTS
Position: Wide Receiver; **Birthdate:** 03.12.58
College: Cal-Poly-SLO; **Height:** 5–8; **Weight:** 177; **NFL Years:** 5

| | | RECEIVING | | | | |
Year	Club	No.	Yds.	Avg.	Lg.	TDs
1981	Detroit	0	0	0.0	0	0
1982	Detroit	1	18	18.0	18	0
1983	Detroit	0	0	0.0	0	0
1984	Detroit	1	9	9.0	9	0
1985	Indianapolis	10	128	12.8	22	0
Totals		**12**	**155**	**12.9**	**22**	**0**

MATHISON, Bruce BUFFALO BILLS
Position: Quarterback; **Birthdate:** 25.04.59
College: Nebraska; **Height:** 6–3; **Weight:** 205; **NFL Years:** 3

| | | PASSING | | | | | | |
Year	Club	Att.	Comp.	Yds.	Lg.	TDs	Int.	Rat.
1983	San Diego	5	3	41	25	0	1	46.7
1984	San Diego	0	0	0	0	0	0	00.0
1985	Buffalo	228	113	1,635	60t	4	14	53.5
Totals		**233**	**116**	**1,676**	**60t**	**4**	**15**	**52.4**

HENRY MARSHALL   ERIC MARTIN

129

MATTHEWS, Allama ATLANTA FALCONS
Position: Tight End; **Birthdate:** 24.08.61
College: Vanderbilt; **Height:** 6–2; **Weight:** 230; **NFL Years:** 3

				RECEIVING		
Year	**Club**	**No.**	**Yds.**	**Avg.**	**Lg.**	**TDs**
1983	Atlanta	3	37	12.3	23	0
1984	Atlanta	1	7	7.0	7	0
1985	Atlanta	7	57	8.1	15	1
Totals		**11**	**101**	**9.2**	**23**	**1**

McCALL, Reese
Position: Tight End; **Birthdate:** 16.06.56
College: Auburn; **Height:** 6–6; **Weight:** 245; **NFL Years:** 8

				RECEIVING		
Year	**Club**	**No.**	**Yds.**	**Avg.**	**Lg.**	**TDs**
1978	Baltimore	11	160	14.5	34	1
1979	Baltimore	37	536	14.5	36	4
1980	Baltimore	18	322	17.9	47	5
1981	Baltimore	21	314	15.0	65t	2
1982	Baltimore	2	6	3.0	4	0
1983	Detroit	1	6	6.0	6	0
1984	Detroit	3	15	5.0	7	0
1985	Detroit	1	7	7.0	7	0
Totals		**94**	**1,366**	**14.5**	**65t**	**12**

McCLOSKEY, Mike HOUSTON OILERS
Position: Tight End; **Birthdate:** 02.02.61
College: Penn State; **Height:** 6–5; **Weight:** 246; **NFL Years:** 3

				RECEIVING		
Year	**Club**	**No.**	**Yds.**	**Avg.**	**Lg.**	**TDs**
1983	Houston	16	137	8.6	20	1
1984	Houston	9	152	16.9	51	1
1985	Houston	4	29	7.3	24t	1
Totals		**29**	**318**	**11.0**	**51**	**3**

BRUCE MATHISON

PHIL McCONKEY

McCONKEY, Phil NEW YORK GIANTS
Position: Wide Receiver; **Birthdate:** 24.02.57
College: Navy; **Height:** 5–10; **Weight:** 170; **NFL Years:** 2

				RECEIVING		
Year	**Club**	**No.**	**Yds.**	**Avg.**	**Lg.**	**TDs**
1983	N.Y. Giants			Did not play		
1984	N.Y. Giants	8	154	19.3	39	0
1985	N.Y. Giants	25	404	16.2	48	1
Totals		**33**	**558**	**16.9**	**48**	**1**

McDONALD, James LOS ANGELES RAMS
Position: Tight End; **Birthdate:** 29.03.61
College: USC; **Height:** 6–5; **Weight:** 230; **NFL Years:** 3

				RECEIVING		
Year	**Club**	**No.**	**Yds.**	**Avg.**	**Lg.**	**TDs**
1983	L.A. Rams	1	1	1.0	1t	1
1984	L.A. Rams	4	55	13.8	22	0
1985	Det.–L.A. Rams	5	81	16.2	35	0
Totals		**10**	**137**	**13.7**	**35**	**1**

McDONALD, Paul CLEVELAND BROWNS
Position: Quarterback; **Birthdate:** 23.02.58
College: USC; **Height:** 6–2; **Weight:** 185; **NFL Years:** 6

		PASSING						
Year	Club	Att.	Comp.	Yds.	Lg.	TDs	Int.	Rat.
1980	Cleveland	0	0	0	0	0	0	00.0
1981	Cleveland	57	35	463	46	4	2	95.8
1982	Cleveland	149	73	993	56t	5	8	59.5
1983	Cleveland	68	32	341	27	1	4	42.6
1984	Cleveland	493	271	3,472	64	14	23	67.3
1985	Cleveland	0	0	0	0	0	0	00.0
Totals		**767**	**411**	**5,269**	**64**	**24**	**37**	**65.7**

McFADDEN, Paul PHILADELPHIA EAGLES
Position: Placekicker; **Birthdate:** 24.09.61
College: Youngstown State; **Height:** 5–11; **Weight:** 155; **NFL Years:** 2

		SCORING					
Year	Club	EPA	EPM	FGA	FGM	Lg.	Pts.
1984	Phildelphia	27	26	37	30	52	116
1985	Philadelphia	29	29	30	25	52	104
Totals		**56**	**55**	**67**	**55**	**52**	**220**

PAUL McDONALD

PAUL McFADDEN

McGEE, Buford SAN DIEGO CHARGERS
Position: Running Back; **Birthdate:** 16.08.60
College: Mississippi; **Height:** 6–0; **Weight:** 203; **NFL Years:** 2

		RUSHING					RECEIVING				
Year	Club	Att.	Yds.	Avg.	Lg.	TDs	No.	Yds.	Avg.	Lg.	TDs
1984	San Diego	67	226	3.4	30	4	9	76	8.4	43	2
1985	San Diego	42	181	4.3	44	3	3	15	5.0	7	0
Totals		**109**	**407**	**3.7**	**44**	**7**	**12**	**91**	**7.6**	**43**	**2**

McGRATH, Mark WASHINGTON REDSKINS
Position: Wide Receiver; **Birthdate:** 17.12.57
College: Montana State; **Height:** 5–11; **Weight:** 175; **NFL Years:** 4

		RECEIVING				
Year	Club	No.	Yds.	Avg.	Lg.	TDs
1980	Seattle			Did not play		
1981	Seattle	4	47	11.8	16	0
1982				Did not play		
1983	Washington	1	6	6.0	6	0
1984	Washington	10	118	11.8	24	1
1985	Washington	0	0	0.0	0	0
Totals		**15**	**171**	**11.4**	**24**	**1**

McIVOR, Rick ST. LOUIS CARDINALS
Position: Quarterback; **Birthdate:** 26.09.60
College: Texas; **Height:** 6–4; **Weight:** 210; **NFL Years:** 2

		PASSING						
Year	Club	Att.	Comp.	Yds.	Lg.	TDs	Int.	Rat.
1984	St. Louis	4	0	0	0	0	0	00.0
1985	St. Louis	0	0	0	0	0	0	00.0
Totals		**4**	**0**	**0**	**0**	**0**	**0**	**00.0**

JIM McMAHON

FREEMAN McNEIL

McKINNON, Dennis CHICAGO BEARS
Position: Wide Receiver; **Birthdate:** 22.08.61
College: Florida State; **Height:** 6–1; **Weight:** 185; **NFL Years:** 3

| | | RECEIVING | | | | |
Year	Club	No.	Yds.	Avg.	Lg.	TDs
1983	Chicago	20	326	16.3	49t	4
1984	Chicago	29	431	14.9	32t	3
1985	Chicago	31	555	17.9	48	7
Totals		**80**	**1,312**	**16.4**	**49t**	**14**

McMAHON, Jim CHICAGO BEARS
Position: Quarterback; **Birthdate:** 21.08.59
College: Brigham Young; **Height:** 6–1; **Weight:** 190; **NFL Years:** 4

| | | PASSING | | | | | | |
Year	Club	Att.	Comp.	Yds.	Lg.	TDs	Int.	Rat.
1982	Chicago	210	120	1,501	50t	9	7	80.1
1983	Chicago	295	175	2,184	87t	12	13	77.6
1984	Chicago	143	85	1,146	61t	8	2	97.8
1985	Chicago	313	178	2,392	70t	15	11	82.6
Totals		**961**	**558**	**7,223**	**87t**	**44**	**33**	**82.7**

McMILLAN, Randy INDIANAPOLIS COLTS
Position: Running Back; **Birthdate:** 17.12.58
College: Pittsburgh; **Height:** 6–0; **Weight:** 212; **NFL Years:** 5

Year	Club	RUSHING					RECEIVING				
		Att.	Yds.	Avg.	Lg.	TDs	No.	Yds.	Avg.	Lg.	TDs
1981	Baltimore	149	597	4.0	42	3	50	466	9.3	31	1
1982	Baltimore	101	305	3.0	13	1	15	90	6.0	17	0
1983	Baltimore	198	802	4.1	39t	5	24	195	8.1	25	1
1984	Indianapolis	163	705	4.3	31	5	19	201	10.6	44	0
1985	Indianapolis	190	858	4.5	38	7	22	115	5.2	17	0
Totals		**801**	**3,267**	**4.1**	**42**	**21**	**130**	**1,067**	**8.2**	**44**	**2**

McNEIL, Freeman NEW YORK JETS
Position: Running Back; **Birthdate:** 22.04.59
College: UCLA; **Height:** 5–11; **Weight:** 212; **NFL Years:** 5

Year	Club	RUSHING					RECEIVING				
		Att.	Yds.	Avg.	Lg.	TDs	No.	Yds.	Avg.	Lg.	TDs
1981	N.Y. Jets	137	623	4.5	43	2	18	171	9.5	18	1
1982	N.Y. Jets	151	786	5.2	48	6	16	187	11.7	32t	1
1983	N.Y. Jets	160	654	4.1	19	1	21	172	8.2	21	3
1984	N.Y. Jets	229	1,070	4.7	53	5	25	294	11.8	32	1
1985	N.Y. Jets	294	1,331	4.5	69	3	38	427	11.2	25	2
Totals		**971**	**4,464**	**4.6**	**69**	**17**	**118**	**1,251**	**10.6**	**32t**	**8**

MEADE, Mike DETROIT LIONS
Position: Running Back; **Birthdate:** 12.02.60
College: Penn State; **Height:** 5–11; **Weight:** 227; **NFL Years:** 4

Year	Club	RUSHING					RECEIVING				
		Att.	Yds.	Avg.	Lg.	TDs	No.	Yds.	Avg.	Lg.	TDs
1982	Green Bay	14	42	3.0	19	0	3	−5	−1.7	−1	0
1983	Green Bay	55	201	3.7	15	1	16	110	6.9	31t	2
1984	Detroit	0	0	0.0	0	0	0	0	0.0	0	0
1985	Detroit	3	18	6.0	9	0	2	21	10.5	14	0
Totals		**72**	**261**	**3.6**	**19**	**1**	**21**	**126**	**6.0**	**31t**	**2**

MERKENS, Guido NEW ORLEANS SAINTS
Position: Wide Receiver; **Birthdate:** 14.08.55
College: Sam Houston State; **Height:** 6–1; **Weight:** 197; **NFL Years:** 8

Year	Club	RECEIVING				
		No.	Yds.	Avg.	Lg.	TDs
1978	Houston	1	6	6.0	6	0
1979	Houston	3	44	14.7	20	1
1980	Hou.–N.O.	0	0	0.0	0	0
1981	New Orleans	29	458	15.8	50	1
1982	New Orleans	0	0	0.0	0	0
1983	New Orleans	0	0	0.0	0	0
1984	New Orleans	0	0	0.0	0	1
1985	New Orleans	3	61	20.3	39t	3
Totals		**36**	**569**	**15.8**	**50**	**3**

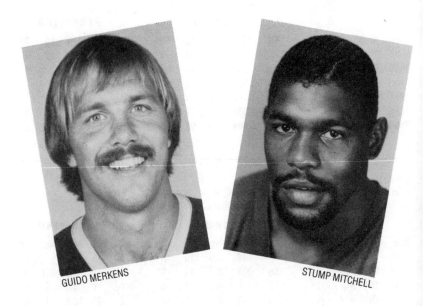

GUIDO MERKENS

STUMP MITCHELL

METZELAARS, Pete BUFFALO BILLS
Position: Tight End; **Birthdate:** 24.05.60
College: Wabash; **Height:** 6–7; **Weight:** 243; **NFL Years:** 4

		RECEIVING				
Year	Club	No.	Yds.	Avg.	Lg.	TDs
1982	Seattle	15	152	10.1	26	0
1983	Seattle	7	72	10.3	17t	1
1984	Seattle	5	80	16.0	25	0
1985	Buffalo	12	80	6.7	13	1
Totals		**39**	**384**	**9.8**	**26**	**2**

MITCHELL, Stump ST. LOUIS CARDINALS
Position: Running Back; **Birthdate:** 15.03.59
College: Citadel; **Height:** 5–9; **Weight:** 188; **NFL Years:** 5

		RUSHING					RECEIVING				
Year	Club	Att.	Yds.	Avg.	Lg.	TDs	No.	Yds.	Avg.	Lg.	TDs
1981	St. Louis	31	175	5.6	43	0	6	35	5.8	16	1
1982	St. Louis	39	189	4.8	32t	1	11	149	13.5	30	0
1983	St. Louis	68	373	5.5	46	3	7	54	7.7	17	0
1984	St. Louis	81	434	5.4	39	9	26	318	12.2	44t	2
1985	St. Louis	183	1,006	5.5	64	7	47	502	10.7	46	3
Totals		**402**	**2,177**	**5.4**	**64**	**20**	**97**	**1,058**	**10.9**	**46**	**6**

MOFFETT, Tim LOS ANGELES RAIDERS
Position: Wide Receiver; **Birthdate:** 28.02.62
College: Mississippi; **Height:** 6–1; **Weight:** 175; **NFL Years:** 1

		RECEIVING				
Year	Club	No.	Yds.	Avg.	Lg.	TDs
1985	L.A. Raiders	5	90	18.0	34	0
Totals		**5**	**90**	**18.0**	**34**	**0**

MONK, Art WASHINGTON REDSKINS
Position: Wide Receiver; **Birthdate:** 05.12.57
College: Syracuse; **Height:** 6–3; **Weight:** 209; **NFL Years:** 6

		RECEIVING				
Year	**Club**	**No.**	**Yds.**	**Avg.**	**Lg.**	**TDs**
1980	Washington	58	797	13.7	54t	3
1981	Washington	56	894	16.0	79t	6
1982	Washington	35	447	12.8	43	1
1983	Washington	47	746	15.9	43t	5
1984	Washington	106	1,372	12.9	72	7
1985	Washington	91	1,226	13.5	53	2
Totals		**393**	**5,482**	**13.9**	**79t**	**24**

MONROE, Carl SAN FRANCISCO 49ers
Position: Running Back; **Birthdate:** 20.02.60
College: Utah; **Height:** 5–8; **Weight:** 180; **NFL Years:** 3

		RUSHING					RECEIVING				
Year	**Club**	**Att.**	**Yds.**	**Avg.**	**Lg.**	**TDs**	**No.**	**Yds.**	**Avg.**	**Lg.**	**TDs**
1983	San Francisco	10	23	2.3	5	0	2	61	30.5	50	0
1984	San Francisco	3	13	4.3	7	0	11	139	12.6	47	1
1985	San Francisco	0	0	0.0	0	0	10	51	5.1	9	0
Totals		**13**	**36**	**2.8**	**7**	**0**	**23**	**251**	**10.9**	**50**	**1**

MONTANA, Joe SAN FRANCISCO 49ers
Position: Quarterback; **Birthdate:** 11.06.56
College: Notre Dame; **Height:** 6–2; **Weight:** 195; **NFL Years:** 7

		PASSING						
Year	**Club**	**Att.**	**Comp.**	**Yds.**	**Lg.**	**TDs**	**Int.**	**Rat.**
1979	San Francisco	23	13	96	18	1	0	80.9
1980	San Francisco	273	176	1,795	71t	15	9	87.8
1981	San Francisco	488	311	3,565	78t	19	12	88.2
1982	San Francisco	346	213	2,613	55	17	11	87.9
1983	San Francisco	515	332	3,910	77t	26	12	94.6
1984	San Francisco	432	279	3,630	80t	28	10	102.9
1985	San Francisco	494	303	3,653	73	27	13	91.3
Totals		**2,571**	**1,627**	**19,262**	**80t**	**133**	**67**	**92.4**

MONTGOMERY, Wilbert DETROIT LIONS
Position: Running Back; **Birthdate:** 16.09.54
College: Abilene Christian; **Height:** 5–10; **Weight:** 194; **NFL Years:** 9

Year	Club	RUSHING Att.	Yds.	Avg.	Lg.	TDs	RECEIVING No.	Yds.	Avg.	Lg.	TDs
1977	Philadelphia	45	183	4.1	27t	2	3	18	6.0	8	0
1978	Philadelphia	259	1,220	4.7	47	9	34	195	5.7	23	1
1979	Philadelphia	338	1,512	4.5	62t	9	41	494	12.0	53t	5
1980	Philadelphia	193	778	4.0	72t	8	50	407	8.1	46	2
1981	Philadelphia	286	1,402	4.9	41	8	49	521	10.6	35t	2
1982	Philadelphia	114	515	4.5	90t	7	20	258	12.9	42t	2
1983	Philadelphia	29	139	4.8	32	0	9	53	5.9	13	0
1984	Philadelphia	201	789	3.9	27	2	60	501	8.4	28	0
1985	Detroit	75	251	3.3	22	0	7	55	7.9	28	0
Totals		**1,540**	**6,789**	**4.4**	**90t**	**45**	**273**	**2,502**	**9.2**	**53t**	**12**

ART MONK   JOE MONTANA

MOON, Warren HOUSTON OILERS
Position: Quarterback; **Birthdate:** 18.11.56
College: Washington; **Height:** 6–3; **Weight:** 208; **NFL Years:** 2

				PASSING				
Year	**Club**	**Att.**	**Comp.**	**Yds.**	**Lg.**	**TDs**	**Int.**	**Rat.**
1984	Houston	450	259	3,338	76	12	14	76.9
1985	Houston	377	200	2,709	80t	15	19	68.5
Totals		**827**	**459**	**6,047**	**80t**	**27**	**33**	**73.1**

MOORE, Alvin DETROIT LIONS
Position: Running Back; **Birthdate:** 03.05.59
College: Arizona State; **Height:** 6–0; **Weight:** 194; **NFL Years:** 3

		RUSHING					RECEIVING				
Year	**Club**	**Att.**	**Yds.**	**Avg.**	**Lg.**	**TDs**	**No.**	**Yds.**	**Avg.**	**Lg.**	**TDs**
1983	Baltimore	57	205	3.6	13	1	6	38	6.3	16	0
1984	Indianapolis	38	127	3.3	18	2	9	52	5.8	12	0
1985	Detroit	80	221	2.8	18	4	19	154	8.1	14	1
Totals		**175**	**553**	**3.2**	**18**	**7**	**34**	**244**	**7.2**	**16**	**1**

WARREN MOON

NAT MOORE

MOORE, Booker BUFFALO BILLS
Position: Running Back; **Birthdate:** 23.06.59
College: Penn State; **Height:** 5–11; **Weight:** 222; **NFL Years:** 4

		RUSHING					RECEIVING				
Year	Club	Att.	Yds.	Avg.	Lg.	TDs	No.	Yds.	Avg.	Lg.	TDs
1981	Buffalo					Did not play					
1982	Buffalo	16	38	2.4	9	0	1	8	8.0	8	0
1983	Buffalo	60	275	4.6	21	0	34	199	5.9	21	1
1984	Buffalo	24	84	3.5	21	0	33	172	5.2	14	0
1985	Buffalo	15	23	1.5	4	1	7	44	6.3	9	0
Totals		**115**	**420**	**3.7**	**21**	**1**	**75**	**423**	**5.6**	**21**	**1**

MOORE, Nat MIAMI DOLPHINS
Position: Wide Receiver; **Birthdate:** 19.09.51
College: Florida; **Height:** 5–9; **Weight:** 188; **NFL Years:** 12

		RECEIVING			
Year	Club	No.	Yds.	Avg.	Lg.	TDs
1974	Miami	37	605	16.4	48	2
1975	Miami	40	705	17.6	70t	4
1976	Miami	33	625	18.9	67t	4
1977	Miami	52	765	14.7	73t	12
1978	Miami	48	645	13.4	47	10
1979	Miami	48	840	17.5	53	6
1980	Miami	47	564	12.0	33	7
1981	Miami	26	452	17.4	52	2
1982	Miami	8	82	10.3	23	1
1983	Miami	39	558	14.3	66t	6
1984	Miami	43	573	13.3	37t	6
1985	Miami	51	701	13.7	69t	7
Totals		**472**	**7,115**	**15.1**	**73t**	**67**

STANLEY MORGAN

JOE MORRIS

MOOREHEAD, Emery CHICAGO BEARS
Position: Tight End; **Birthdate:** 22.03.54
College: Colorado; **Height:** 6–2; **Weight:** 220; **NFL Years:** 9

		RECEIVING				
Year	Club	No.	Yds.	Avg.	Lg.	TDs
1977	N.Y. Giants	12	143	11.9	20	1
1978	N.Y. Giants	3	45	15.0	25	0
1979	N.Y. Giants	9	62	6.9	19	0
1980	Denver	0	0	0.0	0	0
1981	Chicago	0	0	0.0	0	0
1982	Chicago	30	363	12.1	50t	5
1983	Chicago	42	597	14.2	36	3
1984	Chicago	29	497	17.1	50	1
1985	Chicago	35	481	13.7	25	1
Totals		**160**	**2,188**	**13.7**	**50t**	**11**

MORGAN, Stanley NEW ENGLAND PATRIOTS
Position: Wide Receiver; **Birthdate:** 17.02.55
College: Tennessee; **Height:** 5–11; **Weight:** 181; **NFL Years:** 9

				RECEIVING		
Year	Club	No.	Yds.	Avg.	Lg.	TDs
1977	New England	21	443	21.1	64t	3
1978	New England	34	820	24.1	75t	5
1979	New England	44	1,002	22.8	63t	12
1980	New England	45	991	22.0	71	6
1981	New England	44	1,029	23.4	76t	6
1982	New England	28	584	20.9	75t	3
1983	New England	58	863	14.9	50t	2
1984	New England	38	709	18.7	76t	5
1985	New England	39	760	19.5	50t	5
Totals		**351**	**7,201**	**20.5**	**76t**	**47**

MORIARTY, Larry HOUSTON OILERS
Position: Running Back; **Birthdate:** 24.04.58
College: Notre Dame; **Height:** 6–1; **Weight:** 240; **NFL Years:** 3

		RUSHING					RECEIVING				
Year	Club	Att.	Yds.	Avg.	Lg.	TDs	No.	Yds.	Avg.	Lg.	TDs
1983	Houston	65	321	4.9	80	3	4	32	8.0	12	0
1984	Houston	189	785	4.2	51t	6	31	206	6.6	24	1
1985	Houston	106	381	3.6	18	3	17	112	6.6	16	0
Totals		**360**	**1,487**	**4.1**	**80**	**12**	**52**	**350**	**6.7**	**24**	**1**

MORRIS, Joe NEW YORK GIANTS
Position: Running Back; **Birthdate:** 15.09.60
College: Syracuse; **Height:** 5–7; **Weight:** 195; **NFL Years:** 4

		RUSHING					RECEIVING				
Year	Club	Att.	Yds.	Avg.	Lg.	TDs	No.	Yds.	Avg.	Lg.	TDs
1982	N.Y. Giants	15	48	3.2	7	1	8	34	4.3	13	0
1983	N.Y. Giants	35	145	4.1	14	0	2	1	0.5	6t	1
1984	N.Y. Giants	133	510	3.8	28	4	12	124	10.3	26	0
1985	N.Y. Giants	294	1,336	4.5	65t	21	22	212	9.6	17	0
Totals		**477**	**2,093**	**4.4**	**65t**	**26**	**44**	**371**	**8.4**	**26**	**1**

MORRIS, Randall SEATTLE SEAHAWKS
Position: Running Back; **Birthdate:** 22.04.61
College: Tennessee; **Height:** 6–0; **Weight:** 190; **NFL Years:** 2

Year	Club	RUSHING					RECEIVING				
		Att.	Yds.	Avg.	Lg.	TDs	No.	Yds.	Avg.	Lg.	TDs
1984	Seattle	58	189	3.3	16	0	9	61	6.8	18	0
1985	Seattle	55	236	4.3	21	0	6	14	2.3	6	0
Totals		**113**	**425**	**3.8**	**21**	**0**	**15**	**75**	**5.0**	**18**	**0**

MOSELEY, Mark WASHINGTON REDSKINS
Position: Placekicker; **Birthdate:** 12.03.48
College: Stephen F. Austin; **Height:** 6–0; **Weight:** 204; **NFL Years:** 14

Year	Club	SCORING					
		EPA	EPM	FGA	FGM	Lg.	Pts.
1970	Philadelphia	28	25	25	14	42	67
1971	Houston	27	25	26	16	44	73
1972	Houston	2	2	2	1	20	5

RANDALL MORRIS

MARK MOSELEY

Year	Club	EPA	EPM	FGA	FGM	Lg.	Pts.
1973			Did not play				
1974	Washington	30	27	30	18	45	81
1975	Washington	39	37	25	16	48	85
1976	Washington	32	31	34	22	49	97
1977	Washington	19	19	37	21	54	82
1978	Washington	31	30	30	19	52	87
1979	Washington	39	39	33	25	53	114
1980	Washington	30	27	33	18	52	81
1981	Washington	42	38	30	19	49	95
1982	Washington	19	16	21	20	48	76
1983	Washington	63	62	47	33	51	161
1984	Washington	51	48	31	24	51	120
1985	Washington	33	31	34	22	48	97
Totals		**485**	**457**	**438**	**288**	**54**	**1,321**

MOWATT, Zeke NEW YORK GIANTS
Position: Tight End; **Birthdate:** 05.03.61
College: Florida State; **Height:** 6–3; **Weight:** 240; **NFL Years:** 2

			RECEIVING			
Year	Club	No.	Yds.	Avg.	Lg.	TDs
1983	N.Y. Giants	21	280	13.3	46t	1
1984	N.Y. Giants	48	698	14.5	34	6
1985	N.Y. Giants			Did not play		
Totals		**69**	**978**	**14.2**	**46t**	**7**

MUHAMMAD, Calvin WASHINGTON REDSKINS
Position: Wide Receiver; **Birthdate:** 10.12.58
College: Texas Southern; **Height:** 6–0; **Weight:** 190; **NFL Years:** 4

			RECEIVING			
Year	Club	No.	Yds.	Avg.	Lg.	TDs
1981	Oakland			Did not play		
1982	L.A. Raiders	3	92	30.7	43	1
1983	L.A. Raiders	13	252	19.4	45	2
1984	Washington	42	729	17.4	80t	4
1985	Washington	9	116	12.9	32	1
Totals		**67**	**1,189**	**17.7**	**80t**	**8**

145

MULARKEY, Mike MINNESOTA VIKINGS
Position: Tight End; **Birthdate:** 19.11.61
College: Florida; **Height:** 6–4; **Weight:** 233; **NFL Years:** 3

		RECEIVING				
Year	Club	No.	Yds.	Avg.	Lg.	TDs
1983	Minnesota	0	0	0.0	0	0
1984	Minnesota	14	134	9.6	26	2
1985	Minnesota	13	196	15.1	51t	1
Totals		**27**	**330**	**12.2**	**51t**	**3**

MURRAY, Ed DETROIT LIONS
Position: Placekicker; **Birthdate:** 29.08.56
College: Tulane; **Height:** 5–10; **Weight:** 175; **NFL Years:** 6

		SCORING					
Year	Club	EPA	EPM	FGA	FGM	Lg.	Pts.
1980	Detroit	36	35	42	27	52	116
1981	Detroit	46	46	35	25	53	121
1982	Detroit	16	16	12	11	49	49
1983	Detroit	38	38	32	25	54	113
1984	Detroit	31	31	27	20	52	91
1985	Detroit	33	31	31	26	51	109
Totals		**200**	**197**	**179**	**134**	**54**	**599**

NATHAN, Tony MIAMI DOLPHINS
Position: Running Back; **Birthdate:** 14.12.56
College: Alabama; **Height:** 6–0; **Weight:** 206; **NFL Years:** 7

		RUSHING					RECEIVING				
Year	Club	Att.	Yds.	Avg.	Lg.	TDs	No.	Yds.	Avg.	Lg.	TDs
1979	Miami	16	68	4.3	18	0	17	213	12.5	35	2
1980	Miami	60	327	5.5	18	1	57	588	10.3	61	5
1981	Miami	147	782	5.3	46	5	50	452	9.0	31	3
1982	Miami	66	233	3.5	15	1	16	114	7.1	16	0
1983	Miami	151	685	4.5	40	3	52	461	8.9	25	1
1984	Miami	118	558	4.7	22	1	61	579	9.5	26	2
1985	Miami	143	667	4.7	22	5	72	651	9.0	73	1
146 **Totals**		**701**	**3,320**	**4.7**	**46**	**16**	**325**	**3,058**	**9.4**	**73**	**14**

NEHEMIAH, Renaldo
Position: Wide Receiver; **Birthdate:** 24.03.59
College: Maryland; **Height:** 6–1; **Weight:** 177; **NFL Years:** 3

		RECEIVING				
Year	Club	No.	Yds.	Avg.	Lg.	TDs
1982	San Francisco	8	161	20.1	55	1
1983	San Francisco	17	236	13.9	27	1
1984	San Francisco	18	357	19.8	59t	2
1985	San Francisco			Did not play		
Totals		**43**	**754**	**17.5**	**59t**	**4**

NELSON, Darrin MINNESOTA VIKINGS
Position: Running Back; **Birthdate:** 02.01.59
College: Stanford; **Height:** 5–9; **Weight:** 180; **NFL Years:** 4

		RUSHING					RECEIVING				
Year	Club	Att.	Yds.	Avg.	Lg.	TDs	No.	Yds.	Avg.	Lg.	TDs
1982	Minnesota	44	136	3.1	18	0	9	100	11.1	22	0
1983	Minnesota	154	642	4.2	56t	1	51	618	12.1	68	0
1984	Minnesota	80	406	5.1	39	3	27	162	6.0	17	1
1985	Minnesota	200	893	4.5	37	5	43	301	7.0	25t	1
Totals		**478**	**2,077**	**4.3**	**56t**	**9**	**130**	**1,181**	**9.1**	**68**	**2**

ED MURRAY

TONY NATHAN

147

NEWSOME, Ozzie CLEVELAND BROWNS
Position: Tight End; **Birthdate:** 16.03.56
College: Alabama; **Height:** 6–2; **Weight:** 232; **NFL Years:** 8

		RECEIVING				
Year	Club	No.	Yds.	Avg.	Lg.	TDs
1978	Cleveland	38	589	15.5	47	2
1979	Cleveland	55	781	14.2	74	9
1980	Cleveland	51	594	11.6	44	3
1981	Cleveland	69	1,002	14.5	62	6
1982	Cleveland	49	633	12.9	54	3
1983	Cleveland	89	970	10.9	66t	6
1984	Cleveland	89	1,001	11.2	52	5
1985	Cleveland	62	711	11.5	38	5
Totals		**502**	**6,281**	**12.5**	**74**	**39**

NEWSOME, Timmy DALLAS COWBOYS
Position: Running Back; **Birthdate:** 17.05.58
College: Winston-Salem State; **Height:** 6–1; **Weight:** 237; **NFL Years:** 6

		RUSHING					RECEIVING				
Year	Club	Att.	Yds.	Avg.	Lg.	TDs	No.	Yds.	Avg.	Lg.	TDs
1980	Dallas	25	79	3.2	23	2	4	43	10.8	16	0
1981	Dallas	13	38	2.9	7	0	0	0	0.0	0	0
1982	Dallas	15	98	6.5	25	1	6	118	19.7	46t	1
1983	Dallas	44	185	4.2	20	2	18	250	13.9	52t	4
1984	Dallas	66	268	4.1	30	5	26	263	10.1	29	0
1985	Dallas	88	252	2.9	15	2	46	361	7.8	24	1
Totals		**251**	**920**	**3.7**	**30**	**12**	**100**	**1,035**	**10.4**	**52t**	**6**

NICHOLS, Mark DETROIT LIONS
Position: Wide Receiver; **Birthdate:** 29.10.59
College: San Jose State; **Height:** 6–2; **Weight:** 208; **NFL Years:** 5

		RECEIVING				
Year	Club	No.	Yds.	Avg.	Lg.	TDs
1981	Detroit	10	222	22.2	59	1
1982	Detroit	8	146	18.3	48t	2

Year	Club	No.	Yds.	Avg.	Lg.	TDs
1983	Detroit	29	437	15.1	46t	1
1984	Detroit	34	744	21.9	77t	1
1985	Detroit	36	592	16.4	43	4
Totals		**117**	**2,141**	**18.3**	**77t**	**9**

NORWOOD, Scott BUFFALO BILLS
Position: Placekicker; **Birthdate:** 17.07.60
College: James Madison; **Height:** 6–0; **Weight:** 207; **NFL Years:** 1

Year	Club	SCORING					
		EPA	EPM	FGA	FGM	Lg.	Pts.
1985	Buffalo	23	23	17	13	49	62
Totals		**23**	**23**	**17**	**13**	**49**	**62**

OZZIE NEWSOME

MARK NICHOLS

O'BRIEN, Ken NEW YORK JETS
Position: Quarterback; **Birthdate:** 27.11.60
College: California-Davis; **Height:** 6–4; **Weight:** 208; **NFL Years:** 3

				PASSING				
Year	**Club**	**Att.**	**Comp.**	**Yds.**	**Lg.**	**TDs**	**Int.**	**Rat.**
1983	N.Y. Jets	0	0	0	0	0	0	00.0
1984	N.Y. Jets	203	116	1,402	49	6	7	74.0
1985	N.Y. Jets	488	297	3,888	96t	25	8	96.2
Totals		**691**	**413**	**5,290**	**96t**	**31**	**15**	**89.7**

PAGEL, Mike CLEVELAND BROWNS
Position: Quarterback; **Birthdate:** 13.09.60
College: Arizona State; **Height:** 6–2; **Weight:** 207; **NFL Years:** 4

				PASSING				
Year	**Club**	**Att.**	**Comp.**	**Yds.**	**Lg.**	**TDs**	**Int.**	**Rat.**
1982	Baltimore	221	111	1,281	53t	5	7	62.4
1983	Baltimore	328	163	2,353	72t	12	17	64.0

KEN O'BRIEN

STEPHONE PAIGE

Year	Club	Att.	Comp.	Yds.	Lg.	TDs	Int.	Rat.
1984	Indianapolis	212	114	1,426	54t	8	8	71.8
1985	Indianapolis	393	199	2,414	80t	14	15	65.8
Totals		**1,154**	**587**	**7,474**	**80t**	**39**	**47**	**65.8**

PAIGE, Stephone KANSAS CITY CHIEFS
Position: Wide Receiver; **Birthdate:** 15.10.61
College: Fresno State; **Height:** 6–2; **Weight:** 191; **NFL Years:** 3

		RECEIVING				
Year	Club	No.	Yds.	Avg.	Lg.	TDs
1983	Kansas City	30	528	17.6	43	6
1984	Kansas City	30	541	18.0	65t	4
1985	Kansas City	43	943	21.9	84t	10
Totals		**103**	**2,012**	**19.5**	**84t**	**20**

PAIGE, Tony NEW YORK JETS
Position: Running Back; **Birthdate:** 14.10.62
College: Virginia Tech; **Height:** 5–10; **Weight:** 220; **NFL Years:** 2

		RUSHING					RECEIVING				
Year	Club	Att.	Yds.	Avg.	Lg.	TDs	No.	Yds.	Avg.	Lg.	TDs
1984	N.Y. Jets	35	130	3.7	24	7	6	31	5.2	10	1
1985	N.Y. Jets	55	158	2.9	30	8	18	120	6.7	19	2
Totals		**90**	**288**	**3.2**	**30**	**15**	**24**	**151**	**6.3**	**19**	**3**

PARROS, Rick SEATTLE SEAHAWKS
Position: Running Back; **Birthdate:** 14.06.58
College: Utah State; **Height:** 5–11; **Weight:** 200; **NFL Years:** 5

		RUSHING					RECEIVING				
Year	Club	Att.	Yds.	Avg.	Lg.	TDs	No.	Yds.	Avg.	Lg.	TDs
1981	Denver	176	749	4.3	25	2	25	216	8.6	26	1
1982	Denver	77	277	3.6	14	1	37	259	7.0	24	2
1983	Denver	30	96	3.2	13	1	12	126	10.5	33t	2
1984	Denver	46	208	4.5	25	2	6	25	4.2	9	0
1985	Seattle	8	19	2.4	6	0	1	27	27.0	27	0
Totals		**337**	**1,349**	**4.0**	**25**	**6**	**81**	**653**	**8.1**	**33t**	**5**

PAYTON, Walter CHICAGO BEARS
Position: Running Back; **Birthdate:** 25.07.54
College: Jackson State; **Height:** 5–10; **Weight:** 202; **NFL Years:** 11

		RUSHING					RECEIVING				
Year	Club	Att.	Yds.	Avg.	Lg.	TDs	No.	Yds.	Avg.	Lg.	TDs
1975	Chicago	196	679	3.5	54t	7	33	213	6.5	40t	0
1976	Chicago	311	1,390	4.5	60	13	15	149	9.9	34	0
1977	Chicago	339	1,852	5.5	73	14	27	269	10.0	75t	2
1978	Chicago	333	1,395	4.2	76	11	50	480	9.6	61	0
1979	Chicago	369	1,610	4.4	43t	14	31	313	10.1	65t	2
1980	Chicago	317	1,460	4.6	69t	6	46	367	8.0	54t	1
1981	Chicago	339	1,222	3.6	39	6	41	379	9.2	30	2
1982	Chicago	148	596	4.0	26	1	32	311	9.7	40	0
1983	Chicago	314	1,421	4.5	49t	6	53	607	11.5	74t	2
1984	Chicago	381	1,684	4.4	72t	11	45	368	8.2	31	0
1985	Chicago	324	1,551	4.8	40t	9	49	483	9.9	65	2
Totals		**3,371**	**14,860**	**4.4**	**76**	**98**	**422**	**3,939**	**9.3**	**75t**	**11**

PELLUER, Steve DALLAS COWBOYS
Position: Quarterback; **Birthdate:** 29.07.62
College: Washington; **Height:** 6–4; **Weight:** 208; **NFL Years:** 2

		PASSING						
Year	Club	Att.	Comp.	Yds.	Lg.	TDs	Int.	Rat.
1984	Dallas	0	0	0	0	0	0	00.0
1985	Dallas	8	5	47	28	0	0	78.6
Totals		**8**	**5**	**47**	**28**	**0**	**0**	**78.6**

PISARCIK, Joe MIAMI DOLPHINS
Position: Quarterback; **Birthdate:** 02.07.52
College: New Mexico State; **Height:** 6–4; **Weight:** 220; **NFL Years:** 8

		PASSING						
Year	Club	Att.	Comp.	Yds.	Lg.	TDs	Int.	Rat.
1977	N.Y. Giants	241	103	1,346	82	4	14	42.5
1978	N.Y. Giants	301	143	2,096	67t	12	23	52.3
1979	N.Y. Giants	108	43	537	48	2	6	39.0

Year	Club	Att.	Comp.	Yds.	Lg.	TDs	Int.	Rat.
1980	Philadelphia	22	15	187	46	0	0	94.3
1981	Philadelphia	15	8	154	44t	2	2	89.3
1982	Philadelphia	1	1	24	24	0	0	118.8
1983	Philadelphia	34	16	172	33	1	0	72.2
1984	Philadelphia	176	96	1,036	40	3	3	70.6
1985	Miami			Did not play				
Totals		**898**	**425**	**5,552**	**82**	**24**	**48**	**53.9**

PLUNKETT, Jim LOS ANGELES RAIDERS
Position: Quarterback; **Birthdate:** 05.12.47
College: Stanford; **Height:** 6–2; **Weight:** 220; **NFL Years:** 15

PASSING

Year	Club	Att.	Comp.	Yds.	Lg.	TDs	Int.	Rat.
1971	New England	328	158	2,158	88t	19	16	68.6
1972	New England	355	169	2,196	62	8	25	46.1
1973	New England	376	193	2,550	64	13	17	66.0
1974	New England	352	173	2,457	69t	19	22	63.8
1975	New England	92	36	571	76	3	7	39.9
1976	San Francisco	243	126	1,592	85t	13	16	62.8

STEVE PELLUER

JIM PLUNKETT

153

FRANK POLLARD

MIKE QUICK

Year	Club	Att.	Comp.	Yds.	Lg.	TDs	Int.	Rat.
1977	San Francisco	248	128	1,693	47t	9	14	62.2
1978	Oakland	0	0	0	0	0	0	00.0
1979	Oakland	15	7	89	39	1	1	60.1
1980	Oakland	320	165	2,299	86t	18	16	72.8
1981	Oakland	179	94	1,045	42	4	9	56.7
1982	L.A. Raiders	261	152	2,035	52	14	15	77.3
1983	L.A. Raiders	379	230	2,935	99t	20	18	82.7
1984	L.A. Raiders	198	108	1,473	73t	6	10	67.6
1985	L.A. Raiders	103	71	803	41t	3	3	89.6
Totals		**3,449**	**1,810**	**23,896**	**99t**	**150**	**189**	**66.3**

POLLARD, Frank PITTSBURGH STEELERS
Position: Running Back; **Birthdate:** 15.06.57
College: Baylor; **Height:** 5–10; **Weight:** 218; **NFL Years:** 6

		RUSHING					RECEIVING				
Year	Club	Att.	Yds.	Avg.	Lg.	TDs	No.	Yds.	Avg.	Lg.	TDs
1980	Pittsburgh	4	16	4.0	12	0	0	0	0.0	0	0
1981	Pittsburgh	123	570	4.6	29	2	19	156	8.2	26	0
1982	Pittsburgh	62	238	3.8	18	2	6	39	6.5	11	0
1983	Pittsburgh	135	608	4.5	32	4	16	127	7.9	17	0
1984	Pittsburgh	213	851	4.0	52	6	21	186	8.9	18	0
1985	Pittsburgh	233	991	4.3	56	3	24	250	10.4	20	0
Totals		**770**	**3,274**	**4.3**	**56**	**17**	**86**	**758**	**8.8**	**26**	**0**

POWE, Karl DALLAS COWBOYS
Position: Wide Receiver; **Birthdate:** 17.01.62
College: Alabama State; **Height:** 6–2; **Weight:** 175; **NFL Years:** 1

		RECEIVING				
Year	Club	No.	Yds.	Avg.	Lg.	TDs
1985	Dallas	14	237	16.9	34	0
Totals		**14**	**237**	**16.9**	**34**	**0**

PRUITT, Mike KANSAS CITY CHIEFS
Position: Running Back; **Birthdate:** 03.04.54
College: Purdue; **Height:** 6–0; **Weight:** 225; **NFL Years:** 10

		RUSHING					RECEIVING				
Year	Club	Att.	Yds.	Avg.	Lg.	TDs	No.	Yds.	Avg.	Lg.	TDs
1976	Cleveland	52	138	2.7	18	0	8	26	3.3	15	0
1977	Cleveland	47	205	4.4	21	1	3	12	4.0	6	0
1978	Cleveland	135	560	4.1	71t	5	20	112	5.6	15	0
1979	Cleveland	264	1,294	4.9	77t	9	41	372	9.1	50t	2
1980	Cleveland	249	1,034	4.2	56t	6	63	471	7.5	28	0
1981	Cleveland	247	1,103	4.5	21	7	63	442	7.0	21	1
1982	Cleveland	143	516	3.6	17	3	22	140	6.4	13	0
1983	Cleveland	293	1,184	4.0	27	10	30	157	5.2	21	2
1984	Cleveland	163	506	3.1	14	6	5	29	5.8	9	0
1985	Buff.–K.C.	112	390	3.5	54	2	7	43	6.1	9	0
Totals		**1,705**	**6,930**	**4.1**	**77t**	**49**	**262**	**1,804**	**6.9**	**50t**	**5**

QUICK, Mike PHILADELPHIA EAGLES
Position: Wide Receiver; **Birthdate:** 14.05.59
College: North Carolina State; **Height:** 6–2; **Weight:** 190; **NFL Years:** 4

		RECEIVING				
Year	Club	No.	Yds.	Avg.	Lg.	TDs
1982	Philadelphia	10	156	15.6	49t	1
1983	Philadelphia	69	1,409	20.4	83t	13
1984	Philadelphia	61	1,052	17.2	90t	9
1985	Philadelphia	73	1,247	17.1	99t	11
Totals		**213**	**3,864**	**18.1**	**99t**	**34**

RAMSEY, Derrick NEW ENGLAND PATRIOTS
Position: Tight End; **Birthdate:** 23.12.56
College: Kentucky; **Height:** 6–5; **Weight:** 235; **NFL Years:** 8

				RECEIVING		
Year	Club	No.	Yds.	Avg.	Lg.	TDs
1978	Oakland	0	0	0.0	0	0
1979	Oakland	13	161	12.4	40	3
1980	Oakland	5	117	23.4	58	0
1981	Oakland	52	674	13.0	66t	4
1982	L.A. Raiders	0	0	0.0	0	0
1983	L.A.–N.E.	24	335	14.0	39	6
1984	New England	66	792	12.0	34	7
1985	New England	28	285	10.2	26	1
Totals		**188**	**2,364**	**12.6**	**66t**	**21**

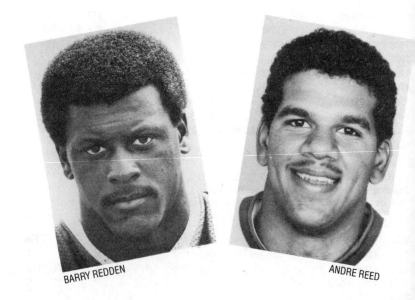

BARRY REDDEN

ANDRE REED

RAMSON, Eason BUFFALO BILLS
Position: Tight End; **Birthdate:** 30.04.56
College: Washington State; **Height:** 6–2; **Weight:** 234; **NFL Years:** 6

		RECEIVING				
Year	Club	No.	Yds.	Avg.	Lg.	TDs
1978	St. Louis	23	238	10.3	26	1
1979	San Francisco	0	0	0.0	0	0
1980	San Francisco	21	179	8.5	22	2
1981	San Francisco	4	45	11.3	16	0
1982	San Francisco	2	27	13.5	21	0
1983	San Francisco	17	125	7.4	16	1
1984	Denver			Did not play		
1985	Buffalo	37	369	10.0	43	1
Totals		**104**	**983**	**9.5**	**43**	**5**

REDDEN, Barry LOS ANGELES RAMS
Position: Running Back; **Birthdate:** 21.07.60
College: Richmond; **Height:** 5–10; **Weight:** 205; **NFL Years:** 4

		RUSHING					RECEIVING				
Year	Club	Att.	Yds.	Avg.	Lg.	TDs	No.	Yds.	Avg.	Lg.	TDs
1982	L.A. Rams	8	24	3.0	7	0	4	16	4.0	11	0
1983	L.A. Rams	75	372	5.0	40t	2	4	30	7.5	9	0
1984	L.A. Rams	45	247	5.5	35	0	4	39	9.8	14	0
1985	L.A. Rams	87	380	4.4	41	0	16	162	10.1	32	0
Totals		**215**	**1,023**	**4.8**	**41**	**2**	**28**	**247**	**8.8**	**32**	**0**

REED, Andre BUFFALO BILLS
Position: Wide Receiver; **Birthdate:** 29.01.64
College: Kutztown State; **Height:** 6–0; **Weight:** 186; **NFL Years:** 1

		RECEIVING				
Year	Club	No.	Yds.	Avg.	Lg.	TDs
1985	Buffalo	48	637	13.3	32	4
Totals		**48**	**637**	**13.3**	**32**	**4**

157

MIKE RENFRO

JERRY RICE

RENFRO, Mike DALLAS COWBOYS
Position: Wide Receiver; **Birthdate:** 19.06.55
College: Texas Christian; **Height:** 6–0; **Weight:** 189; **NFL Years:** 8

			RECEIVING			
Year	Club	No.	Yds.	Avg.	Lg.	TDs
1978	Houston	26	339	13.0	58t	2
1979	Houston	16	323	20.2	49	2
1980	Houston	35	459	13.1	42	1
1981	Houston	39	451	11.6	43	1
1982	Houston	21	295	14.0	54t	3
1983	Houston	23	316	13.7	38t	2
1984	Dallas	35	583	16.7	60t	2
1985	Dallas	60	955	15.9	58t	8
Totals		**255**	**3,721**	**14.6**	**60t**	**21**

REVEIZ, Fuad MIAMI DOLPHINS
Position: Placekicker; **Birthdate:** 04.02.63
College: Tennessee; **Height:** 5–11; **Weight:** 222; **NFL Years:** 1

		SCORING					
Year	Club	EPA	EPM	FGA	FGM	Lg.	Pts.
1985	Miami	52	50	27	22	49	116
Totals		**52**	**50**	**27**	**22**	**49**	**116**

RICE, Allen MINNESOTA VIKINGS
Position: Running Back; **Birthdate:** 05.04.62
College: Baylor; **Height:** 5–10; **Weight:** 198; **NFL Years:** 2

		RUSHING					RECEIVING				
Year	Club	Att.	Yds.	Avg.	Lg.	TDs	No.	Yds.	Avg.	Lg.	TDs
1984	Minnesota	14	58	4.1	16	1	4	59	14.8	24	1
1985	Minnesota	31	104	3.4	15	3	9	61	6.8	13	1
Totals		**45**	**162**	**3.6**	**16**	**4**	**13**	**120**	**9.2**	**24**	**2**

RICE, Jerry SAN FRANCISCO 49ers
Position: Wide Receiver; **Birthdate:** 13.10.62
College: Mississippi Valley St.; **Height:** 6–2; **Weight:** 200; **NFL Years:** 1

		RECEIVING				
Year	Club	No.	Yds.	Avg.	Lg.	TDs
1985	San Francisco	49	927	18.9	66t	3
Totals		**49**	**927**	**18.9**	**66t**	**3**

RICHARDSON, Eric BUFFALO BILLS
Position: Wide Receiver; **Birthdate:** 18.04.62
College: San Jose State; **Height:** 6–1; **Weight:** 185; **NFL Years:** 1

		RECEIVING				
Year	Club	No.	Yds.	Avg.	Lg.	TDs
1984	Buffalo			Did not play		
1985	Buffalo	12	201	16.8	27	0
Totals		**12**	**201**	**16.8**	**27**	**0**

RIGGINS, John WASHINGTON REDSKINS
Position: Running Back; **Birthdate:** 04.08.49
College: Kansas; **Height:** 6–2; **Weight:** 240; **NFL Years:** 14

| Year | Club | RUSHING | | | | | RECEIVING | | | | |
		Att.	Yds.	Avg.	Lg.	TDs	No.	Yds.	Avg.	Lg.	TDs
1971	N.Y. Jets	180	769	4.3	25	1	36	231	6.4	32	2
1972	N.Y. Jets	207	944	4.6	40	7	21	230	11.0	67t	1
1973	N.Y. Jets	134	482	3.6	15	4	23	158	6.9	19	0
1974	N.Y. Jets	169	680	4.0	34	5	19	180	9.5	32	2
1975	N.Y. Jets	238	1,005	4.2	42	8	30	363	12.1	34	1
1976	Washington	162	572	3.5	15	3	21	172	8.2	18	1
1977	Washington	68	203	3.0	12	0	7	95	13.6	53	2
1978	Washington	248	1,014	4.1	31	5	31	299	9.6	33	0
1979	Washington	260	1,153	4.4	66t	9	28	163	5.8	23	3
1980	Washington				Did not play						
1981	Washington	195	714	3.7	24	13	6	59	9.8	22	0
1982	Washington	177	553	3.1	19	3	10	50	5.0	11	0
1983	Washington	375	1,347	3.6	44	24	5	29	5.8	14	0
1984	Washington	327	1,239	3.8	24	14	7	43	6.1	11	0
1985	Washington	176	677	3.8	51	8	6	18	3.0	8	0
Totals		**2,916**	**11,352**	**3.9**	**66t**	**104**	**250**	**2,090**	**8.4**	**67t**	**12**

GERALD RIGGS

BILL RING

RIGGS, Gerald ATLANTA FALCONS
Position: Running Back; **Birthdate:** 06.11.60
College: Arizona State; **Height:** 6–1; **Weight:** 230; **NFL Years:** 4

Year	Club	RUSHING					RECEIVING				
		Att.	Yds.	Avg.	Lg.	TDs	No.	Yds.	Avg.	Lg.	TDs
1982	Atlanta	78	299	3.8	37	5	23	185	8.0	15	0
1983	Atlanta	100	437	4.4	40t	8	17	149	8.8	25	0
1984	Atlanta	353	1,486	4.2	57	13	42	277	6.6	21	0
1985	Atlanta	397	1,719	4.3	50	10	33	267	8.1	44	0
Totals		**928**	**3,941**	**4.2**	**57**	**36**	**115**	**878**	**7.6**	**44**	**0**

RING, Bill SAN FRANCISCO 49ers
Position: Running Back; **Birthdate:** 13.12.56
College: Brigham Young; **Height:** 5–10; **Weight:** 205; **NFL Years:** 5

Year	Club	RUSHING					RECEIVING				
		Att.	Yds.	Avg.	Lg.	TDs	No.	Yds.	Avg.	Lg.	TDs
1981	San Francisco	22	106	4.8	16	0	3	28	9.3	21	1
1982	San Francisco	48	183	3.8	11	1	13	94	7.2	15	0
1983	San Francisco	64	254	4.0	25	2	23	182	7.9	24	0
1984	San Francisco	38	162	4.3	34	3	3	10	3.3	15	0
1985	San Francisco	8	23	2.9	9t	1	2	14	7.0	8	0
Totals		**180**	**728**	**4.0**	**34**	**7**	**44**	**328**	**7.5**	**24**	**1**

RODGERS, Del GREEN BAY PACKERS
Position: Running Back; **Birthdate:** 22.06.60
College: Utah; **Height:** 5–10; **Weight:** 202; **NFL Years:** 2

Year	Club	RUSHING					RECEIVING				
		Att.	Yds.	Avg.	Lg.	TDs	No.	Yds.	Avg.	Lg.	TDs
1982	Green Bay	46	175	3.8	13	1	3	23	7.7	16	0
1983	Green Bay					Did not play					
1984	Green Bay	25	94	3.8	15	0	5	56	11.2	22	0
1985	Green Bay					Did not play					
Totals		**71**	**269**	**3.8**	**15**	**1**	**8**	**79**	**9.9**	**22**	**0**

ROGERS, George WASHINGTON REDSKINS
Position: Running Back; **Birthdate:** 08.12.58
College: South Carolina; **Height:** 6–2; **Weight:** 225; **NFL Years:** 5

		RUSHING					RECEIVING				
Year	Club	Att.	Yds.	Avg.	Lg.	TDs	No.	Yds.	Avg.	Lg.	TDs
1981	New Orleans	378	1,674	4.4	79t	13	16	126	7.9	25	0
1982	New Orleans	122	535	4.4	38	3	4	21	5.3	10	0
1983	New Orleans	256	1,144	4.5	76t	5	12	69	5.8	22	0
1984	New Orleans	239	914	3.8	28	2	12	76	6.3	15	0
1985	Washington	231	1,093	4.7	35	7	4	29	7.3	23	0
Totals		**1,226**	**5,360**	**4.4**	**79t**	**30**	**48**	**321**	**6.7**	**25**	**0**

ROSE, Joe MIAMI DOLPHINS
Position: Tight End; **Birthdate:** 24.06.57
College: California; **Height:** 6–3; **Weight:** 230; **NFL Years:** 6

		RECEIVING				
Year	Club	No.	Yds.	Avg.	Lg.	TDs
1980	Miami	13	149	11.5	50	0
1981	Miami	23	316	13.7	50	2
1982	Miami	16	182	11.4	44	2
1983	Miami	29	345	11.9	37	3
1984	Miami	12	195	16.3	34t	2
1985	Miami	19	306	16.1	42	4
Totals		**112**	**1,493**	**13.3**	**50**	**13**

ROSS, Dan SEATTLE SEAHAWKS
Position: Tight End; **Birthdate:** 09.02.57
College: Northeastern; **Height:** 6–4; **Weight:** 235; **NFL Years:** 6

		RECEIVING				
Year	Club	No.	Yds.	Avg.	Lg.	TDs
1979	Cincinnati	41	516	12.6	41	1
1980	Cincinnati	56	724	12.9	37	4
1981	Cincinnati	71	910	12.8	37	5
1982	Cincinnati	47	508	10.8	28	3
1983	Cincinnati	42	483	11.5	30	3

Year	Club	No.	Yds.	Avg.	Lg.	TDs
1984				Did not play		
1985	Cin.–Seattle	16	135	8.4	20	2
Totals		**273**	**3,276**	**12.0**	**41**	**18**

ROZIER, Mike HOUSTON OILERS
Position: Running Back; **Birthdate:** 01.03.61
College: Nebraska; **Height:** 5–10; **Weight:** 198; **NFL Years:** 1

			RUSHING					RECEIVING			
Year	Club	Att.	Yds.	Avg.	Lg.	TDs	No.	Yds.	Avg.	Lg.	TDs
1985	Houston	133	462	3.5	30	8	9	96	10.7	52	0
Totals		**133**	**462**	**3.5**	**30**	**8**	**9**	**96**	**10.7**	**52**	**0**

RUBICK, Rob DETROIT LIONS
Position: Tight End; **Birthdate:** 27.09.60
College: Grand Valley State; **Height:** 6–3; **Weight:** 234; **NFL Years:** 4

				RECEIVING		
Year	Club	No.	Yds.	Avg.	Lg.	TDs
1982	Detroit	0	0	0.0	0	0
1983	Detroit	10	81	8.1	15	1
1984	Detroit	14	188	13.4	29	1
1985	Detroit	2	33	16.5	18	0
Totals		**26**	**302**	**11.6**	**29**	**2**

GEORGE ROGERS

MIKE ROZIER

163

CLINT SAMPSON

THOMAS SANDERS

RUTLEDGE, Jeff NEW YORK GIANTS
Position: Quarterback; **Birthdate:** 22.01.57
College: Alabama; **Height:** 6–1; **Weight:** 195; **NFL Years:** 7

		PASSING						
Year	**Club**	**Att.**	**Comp.**	**Yds.**	**Lg.**	**TDs**	**Int.**	**Rat.**
1979	L.A. Rams	32	13	125	22	1	4	23.0
1980	L.A. Rams	4	1	26	26	0	0	54.2
1981	L.A. Rams	50	30	442	64	3	4	75.6
1982	N.Y. Giants	0	0	0	0	0	0	00.0
1983	N.Y. Giants	174	87	1,208	54	3	8	59.3
1984	N.Y. Giants	1	1	9	9	0	0	104.2
1985	N.Y. Giants	0	0	0	0	0	0	00.0
Totals		**261**	**132**	**1,810**	**64**	**7**	**16**	**56.5**

RYAN, Pat NEW YORK JETS
Position: Quarterback; **Birthdate:** 16.09.55
College: Tennessee; **Height:** 6–3; **Weight:** 210; **NFL Years:** 8

		PASSING						
Year	**Club**	**Att.**	**Comp.**	**Yds.**	**Lg.**	**TDs**	**Int.**	**Rat.**
1978	N.Y. Jets	14	9	106	18	0	2	47.6
1979	N.Y. Jets	4	2	13	7	0	1	17.7

Year	Club	Att.	Comp.	Yds.	Lg.	TDs	Int.	Rat.
1980	N.Y. Jets	0	0	0	0	0	0	00.0
1981	N.Y. Jets	10	4	48	18	1	1	49.2
1982	N.Y. Jets	18	12	146	20t	2	1	105.1
1983	N.Y. Jets	40	21	259	36	2	2	68.6
1984	N.Y. Jets	285	156	1,939	44t	14	14	72.0
1985	N.Y. Jets	9	6	95	50	0	0	101.6
Totals		**380**	**210**	**2,606**	**50**	**19**	**21**	**70.4**

SAMPSON, Clint DENVER BRONCOS
Position: Wide Receiver; **Birthdate:** 04.01.61
College: San Diego State; **Height:** 5–11; **Weight:** 183; **NFL Years:** 3

		RECEIVING				
Year	Club	No.	Yds.	Avg.	Lg.	TDs
1983	Denver	10	200	20.0	49t	3
1984	Denver	9	123	13.7	25	1
1985	Denver	26	432	16.6	46	4
Totals		**45**	**755**	**16.8**	**49t**	**8**

SANDERS, Thomas CHICAGO BEARS
Position: Running Back; **Birthdate:** 04.01.62
College: Texas A&M; **Height:** 5–11; **Weight:** 203; **NFL Years:** 1

		RUSHING					RECEIVING				
Year	Club	Att.	Yds.	Avg.	Lg.	TDs	No.	Yds.	Avg.	Lg.	TDs
1985	Chicago	25	104	4.2	28	1	1	9	9.0	9	0
Totals		**25**	**104**	**4.2**	**28**	**1**	**1**	**9**	**9.0**	**9**	**0**

SAWYER, John DENVER BRONCOS
Position: Tight End; **Birthdate:** 26.07.53
College: Southern Mississippi; **Height:** 6–2; **Weight:** 230; **NFL Years:** 9

		RECEIVING				
Year	Club	No.	Yds.	Avg.	Lg.	TDs
1975	Houston	7	144	20.6	51	1
1976	Houston	18	208	11.6	53	1
1977	Seattle	10	105	10.5	27	0

Year	Club	No.	Yds.	Avg.	Lg.	TDs
1978	Seattle	9	101	11.2	20	0
1979	Seattle			Did not play		
1980	Seattle	36	410	11.4	32	0
1981	Seattle	21	272	13.0	30	0
1982	Seattle	8	92	11.5	17	0
1983	Wash.–Den.	3	42	14.0	17	0
1984	Denver	17	122	7.2	25	0
1985	Denver			Did not play		
Totals		**129**	**1,496**	**11.6**	**53**	**2**

SCHONERT, Turk ATLANTA FALCONS
Position: Quarterback; **Birthdate:** 15.01.57
College: Stanford; **Height:** 6–1; **Weight:** 190; **NFL Years:** 6

				PASSING				
Year	Club	Att.	Comp.	Yds.	Lg.	TDs	Int.	Rat.
1980	Cincinnati	0	0	0	0	0	0	00.0
1981	Cincinnati	19	10	166	36	0	0	82.3

JOHN SAWYER   JAY SCHROEDER

Year	Club	Att.	Comp.	Yds.	Lg.	TDs	Int.	Rat.
1982	Cincinnati	1	1	6	6	0	0	91.7
1983	Cincinnati	156	92	1,159	54	2	5	73.1
1984	Cincinnati	117	78	945	57t	4	7	77.8
1985	Cincinnati	51	33	460	71	1	0	100.1
Totals		**344**	**214**	**2,736**	**71**	**7**	**12**	**79.3**

SCHROEDER, Jay WASHINGTON REDSKINS
Position: Quarterback; **Birthdate:** 28.06.61
College: UCLA; **Height:** 6–4; **Weight:** 215; **NFL Years:** 2

				PASSING				
Year	Club	Att.	Comp.	Yds.	Lg.	TDs	Int.	Rat.
1984	Washington	0	0	0	0	0	0	00.0
1985	Washington	209	112	1,458	53	5	5	73.8
Totals		**209**	**112**	**1,458**	**53**	**5**	**5**	**73.8**

SCHUBERT, Eric NEW YORK GIANTS
Position: Placekicker; **Birthdate:** 28.05.62
College: Pittsburgh; **Height:** 5–8; **Weight:** 193; **NFL Years:** 1

				SCORING			
Year	Club	EPA	EPM	FGA	FGM	Lg.	Pts.
1985	N.Y. Giants	27	26	13	10	41	56
Totals		**27**	**26**	**13**	**10**	**41**	**56**

SCOTT, Willie KANSAS CITY CHIEFS
Position: Tight End; **Birthdate:** 13.02.59
College: South Carolina; **Height:** 6–4; **Weight:** 254; **NFL Years:** 5

			RECEIVING		
Year	Club	No.	Yds.	Avg.	Lg.	TDs
1981	Kansas City	5	72	14.4	26	1
1982	Kansas City	8	49	6.1	13	1
1983	Kansas City	29	247	8.5	22	6
1984	Kansas City	28	253	9.0	27	3
1985	Kansas City	5	61	12.2	21	0
Totals		**75**	**682**	**9.1**	**27**	**11**

SEPTIEN, Rafael DALLAS COWBOYS
Position: Placekicker; **Birthdate:** 12.12.53
College: S.W. Louisiana; **Height:** 5–10; **Weight:** 179; **NFL Years:** 9

		SCORING					
Year	Club	EPA	EPM	FGA	FGM	Lg.	Pts.
1977	L.A. Rams	35	32	30	18	45	86
1978	Dallas	47	46	26	16	48	94
1979	Dallas	44	40	29	19	51	97
1980	Dallas	60	59	17	11	52	92
1981	Dallas	40	40	35	27	47	121
1982	Dallas	28	28	14	10	53	58
1983	Dallas	59	57	27	22	47	123
1984	Dallas	34	33	29	23	52	102
1985	Dallas	43	42	28	19	53	99
Totals		**390**	**377**	**235**	**165**	**53**	**872**

SEWELL, Steve DENVER BRONCOS
Position: Running Back; **Birthdate:** 02.04.63
College: Oklahoma; **Height:** 6–3; **Weight:** 210; **NFL Years:** 1

		RUSHING					RECEIVING				
Year	Club	Att.	Yds.	Avg.	Lg.	TDs	No.	Yds.	Avg.	Lg.	TDs
1985	Denver	81	275	3.4	16	4	24	224	9.3	54t	1
Totals		**81**	**275**	**3.4**	**16**	**4**	**24**	**224**	**9.3**	**54t**	**1**

SHERWIN, Tim INDIANAPOLIS COLTS
Position: Tight End; **Birthdate:** 04.05.58
College: Boston College; **Height:** 6–6; **Weight:** 243; **NFL Years:** 5

		RECEIVING				
Year	Club	No.	Yds.	Avg.	Lg.	TDs
1981	Baltimore	2	19	9.5	11	0
1982	Baltimore	21	280	13.3	33	0
1983	Baltimore	25	358	14.3	30	0
1984	Indianapolis	11	169	15.4	26	0
1985	Indianapolis	5	64	12.8	29	0
Totals		**64**	**890**	**13.9**	**33**	**0**

RAFAEL SEPTIEN

MICKEY SHULER

SHULER, Mickey NEW YORK JETS
Position: Tight End; **Birthdate:** 21.08.56
College: Penn State; **Height:** 6–3; **Weight:** 231; **NFL Years:** 8

		RECEIVING				
Year	Club	No.	Yds.	Avg.	Lg.	TDs
1978	N.Y. Jets	11	67	6.1	15	3
1979	N.Y. Jets	16	225	14.1	46	3
1980	N.Y. Jets	22	226	10.3	26	2
1981	N.Y. Jets	0	0	0.0	0	0
1982	N.Y. Jets	8	132	16.5	51	3
1983	N.Y. Jets	26	272	10.5	28	1
1984	N.Y. Jets	68	782	11.5	49	6
1985	N.Y. Jets	76	879	11.6	35	7
Totals		227	2,583	11.4	51	25

169

SIEVERS, Eric SAN DIEGO CHARGERS
Position: Tight End; **Birthdate:** 09.11.58
College: Maryland; **Height:** 6–3; **Weight:** 236; **NFL Years:** 5

		RECEIVING				
Year	Club	No.	Yds.	Avg.	Lg.	TDs
1981	San Diego	22	276	12.5	32	3
1982	San Diego	12	173	14.4	26	1
1983	San Diego	33	452	13.7	28	3
1984	San Diego	41	438	10.7	32	3
1985	San Diego	41	438	10.7	30t	6
Totals		**149**	**1,777**	**11.9**	**32**	**16**

SIMMS, Phil NEW YORK GIANTS
Position: Quarterback; **Birthdate:** 03.11.55
College: Morehead State; **Height:** 6–3; **Weight:** 214; **NFL Years:** 6

		PASSING						
Year	Club	Att.	Comp.	Yds.	Lg.	TDs	Int.	Rat.
1979	N.Y. Giants	265	134	1,743	61	13	14	65.9
1980	N.Y. Giants	402	193	2,321	58t	15	19	58.9
1981	N.Y. Giants	316	172	2,031	80	11	9	74.2

ERIC SIEVERS

PHIL SIMMS

Year	Club	Att.	Comp.	Yds.	Lg.	TDs	Int.	Rat.
982	N.Y. Giants			Did not play				
983	N.Y. Giants	13	7	130	36	0	1	56.6
984	N.Y. Giants	533	286	4,044	65t	22	18	78.1
985	N.Y. Giants	495	275	3,829	70t	22	20	78.6
otals		**2,024**	**1,067**	**14,098**	**80**	**83**	**81**	**72.0**

SIMS, Billy DETROIT LIONS
Position: Running Back; **Birthdate:** 18.09.55
College: Oklahoma; **Height:** 6–0; **Weight:** 212; **NFL Years:** 5

		RUSHING					RECEIVING				
Year	Club	Att.	Yds.	Avg.	Lg.	TDs	No.	Yds.	Avg.	Lg.	TDs
980	Detroit	313	1,303	4.2	52	13	51	621	12.2	87t	3
981	Detroit	296	1,437	4.9	51	13	28	451	16.1	81t	2
982	Detroit	172	639	3.7	29	4	34	342	10.1	52	0
983	Detroit	220	1,040	4.7	41	7	42	419	10.0	54	0
984	Detroit	130	687	5.3	81	5	31	239	7.7	20	0
985	Detroit			Did not play							
otals		**1,131**	**5,106**	**4.5**	**81**	**42**	**186**	**2,072**	**11.1**	**87t**	**5**

SKANSI, Paul SEATTLE SEAHAWKS
Position: Wide Receiver; **Birthdate:** 11.01.61
College: Washington; **Height:** 5–11; **Weight:** 190; **NFL Years:** 3

		RECEIVING			
Year	Club	No.	Yds.	Avg.	Lg.	TDs
983	Pittsburgh	3	39	13.0	21	0
984	Seattle	7	85	12.1	27	0
985	Seattle	21	269	12.8	32	1
otals		**31**	**393**	**12.7**	**32**	**1**

SMITH, Jeff KANSAS CITY CHIEFS
Position: Running Back; **Birthdate:** 22.03.62
College: Nebraska; **Height:** 5–9; **Weight:** 201; **NFL Years:** 1

		RUSHING					RECEIVING				
Year	Club	Att.	Yds.	Avg.	Lg.	TDs	No.	Yds.	Avg.	Lg.	TDs
985	Kansas City	30	118	3.9	27	0	18	157	8.7	45t	2
otals		**30**	**118**	**3.9**	**27**	**0**	**18**	**157**	**8.7**	**45t**	**2**

J.T. SMITH

TIM SMITH

SMITH, Jim
Position: Wide Receiver; **Birthdate:** 20.07.55
College: Michigan; **Height:** 6–2; **Weight:** 195; **NFL Years:** 7

| | | | | RECEIVING | | |
Year	Club	No.	Yds.	Avg.	Lg.	TDs
1977	Pittsburgh	4	80	20.0	26	0
1978	Pittsburgh	6	83	13.8	29t	2
1979	Pittsburgh	17	243	14.3	25	2
1980	Pittsburgh	37	711	19.2	45t	9
1981	Pittsburgh	29	571	19.7	46t	7
1982	Pittsburgh	17	387	22.8	51	4
1983				Did not play		
1984				Did not play		
1985	L.A. Raiders	3	28	9.3	14	1
Totals		**113**	**2,103**	**18.6**	**51**	**25**

SMITH, J.T. ST. LOUIS CARDINALS
Position: Wide Receiver; **Birthdate:** 29.10.55
. **College:** North Texas State; **Height:** 6–2; **Weight:** 185; **NFL Years:** 8

| | | | | RECEIVING | | |
Year	Club	No.	Yds.	Avg.	Lg.	TDs
1978	Wash.–K.C.	0	0	0.0	0	0
1979	Kansas City	33	444	13.5	34	3

Year	Club	No.	Yds.	Avg.	Lg.	TDs
1980	Kansas City	46	655	14.2	77	2
1981	Kansas City	63	852	13.5	42	2
1982	Kansas City	10	168	16.8	51	1
1983	Kansas City	7	85	12.1	18	0
1984	Kansas City	8	69	8.6	16	0
1985	St. Louis	43	581	13.5	34	1
Totals		**210**	**2,854**	**13.6**	**77**	**9**

SMITH, Tim HOUSTON OILERS
Position: Wide Receiver; **Birthdate:** 20.03.57
College: Nebraska; **Height:** 6–2; **Weight:** 206; **NFL Years:** 6

Year	Club	RECEIVING				
		No.	Yds.	Avg.	Lg.	TDs
1980	Houston	2	21	10.5	13	0
1981	Houston	2	37	18.5	25	0
1982	Houston	0	0	0.0	0	0
1983	Houston	83	1,176	14.2	47t	6
1984	Houston	69	1,141	16.5	75t	4
1985	Houston	46	660	14.3	33	2
Totals		**202**	**3,035**	**15.0**	**75t**	**12**

SOHN, Kurt NEW YORK JETS
Position: Wide Receiver; **Birthdate:** 26.06.57
College: Fordham; **Height:** 5–11; **Weight:** 180; **NFL Years:** 4

Year	Club	RECEIVING				
		No.	Yds.	Avg.	Lg.	TDs
1981	N.Y. Jets	0	0	0.0	0	0
1982	N.Y. Jets	0	0	0.0	0	0
1983	N.Y. Jets			Did not play		
1984	N.Y. Jets	2	28	14.0	16	0
1985	N.Y. Jets	39	534	13.7	39t	4
Totals		**41**	**562**	**13.7**	**39t**	**4**

SPAGNOLA, John PHILADELPHIA EAGLES
Position: Tight End; **Birthdate:** 01.08.57
College: Yale; **Height:** 6–4; **Weight:** 238; **NFL Years:** 6

		RECEIVING				
Year	Club	No.	Yds.	Avg.	Lg.	TDs
1979	Philadelphia	2	24	12.0	14	0
1980	Philadelphia	18	193	10.7	20	3
1981	Philadelphia	6	83	13.8	28	0
1982	Philadelphia	26	313	12.0	57	2
1983	Philadelphia			Did not play		
1984	Philadelphia	65	701	10.8	34	1
1985	Philadelphia	64	772	12.1	35	5
Totals		**181**	**2,086**	**11.5**	**57**	**11**

SPENCER, Tim SAN DIEGO CHARGERS
Position: Running Back; **Birthdate:** 10.12.60
College: Ohio State; **Height:** 6–1; **Weight:** 220; **NFL Years:** 1

		RUSHING					RECEIVING				
Year	Club	Att.	Yds.	Avg.	Lg.	TDs	No.	Yds.	Avg.	Lg.	TDs
1985	San Diego	124	478	3.9	24	10	11	135	12.3	43	0
Totals		**124**	**478**	**3.9**	**24**	**10**	**11**	**135**	**12.3**	**43**	**0**

SPENCER, Todd PITTSBURGH STEELERS
Position: Running Back; **Birthdate:** 26.07.62
College: USC; **Height:** 6–0; **Weight:** 217; **NFL Years:** 2

		RUSHING					RECEIVING				
Year	Club	Att.	Yds.	Avg.	Lg.	TDs	No.	Yds.	Avg.	Lg.	TDs
1984	Pittsburgh	1	0	0.0	0	0	0	0	0.0	0	0
1985	Pittsburgh	13	56	4.3	11	0	3	25	8.3	13	0
Totals		**14**	**56**	**4.3**	**11**	**0**	**3**	**25**	**8.3**	**13**	**0**

SPRINGS, Ron TAMPA BAY BUCCANEERS
Position: Running Back; **Birthdate:** 01.11.56
College: Ohio State; **Height:** 6–1; **Weight:** 224; **NFL Years:** 7

		RUSHING					RECEIVING				
Year	Club	Att.	Yds.	Avg.	Lg.	TDs	No.	Yds.	Avg.	Lg.	TDs
1979	Dallas	67	248	3.7	15	2	25	251	10.0	27	1
1980	Dallas	89	326	3.7	20t	6	15	212	14.1	58t	1
1981	Dallas	172	625	3.6	16	10	46	359	7.8	32t	2
1982	Dallas	59	243	4.1	46t	2	17	163	9.6	34	2
1983	Dallas	149	541	3.6	19t	7	73	589	8.1	80t	1
1984	Dallas	68	197	2.9	16	1	46	454	9.9	57t	3
1985	Tampa Bay	16	54	3.4	11	0	3	44	14.7	22	0
Totals		**620**	**2,234**	**3.6**	**46t**	**28**	**225**	**2,072**	**9.2**	**80t**	**10**

JOHN SPAGNOLA

TIM SPENCER

STALLWORTH, John PITTSBURGH STEELERS
Position: Wide Receiver; **Birthdate:** 15.07.52
College: Alabama A&M; **Height:** 6–2; **Weight:** 202; **NFL Years:** 12

		RECEIVING				
Year	Club	No.	Yds.	Avg.	Lg.	TDs
1974	Pittsburgh	16	269	16.8	56	1
1975	Pittsburgh	20	423	21.2	59	4
1976	Pittsburgh	9	111	12.3	25	2
1977	Pittsburgh	44	784	17.8	49t	7
1978	Pittsburgh	41	798	19.5	70	9
1979	Pittsburgh	70	1,183	16.9	65t	8
1980	Pittsburgh	9	197	21.9	50t	1
1981	Pittsburgh	63	1,098	17.4	55	5
1982	Pittsburgh	27	441	16.3	74t	7
1983	Pittsburgh	8	100	12.5	20	0
1984	Pittsburgh	80	1,395	17.4	51	11
1985	Pittsburgh	75	937	12.5	41	5
Totals		**462**	**7,736**	**16.7**	**74t**	**60**

JOHN STALLWORTH

DON STROCK

STARRING, Stephen NEW ENGLAND PATRIOTS
Position: Wide Receiver; **Birthdate:** 30.07.61
College: McNeese State; **Height:** 5–10; **Weight:** 172; **NFL Years:** 3

		RECEIVING				
Year	**Club**	**No.**	**Yds.**	**Avg.**	**Lg.**	**TDs**
1983	New England	17	389	22.9	76t	2
1984	New England	46	657	14.3	65t	4
1985	New England	16	235	14.7	40	0
Totals		**79**	**1,281**	**16.2**	**76t**	**6**

STEELS, Anthony BUFFALO BILLS
Position: Running Back; **Birthdate:** 08.01.59
College: Nebraska; **Height:** 5–9; **Weight:** 200; **NFL Years:** 1

		RUSHING					**RECEIVING**				
Year	**Club**	**Att.**	**Yds.**	**Avg.**	**Lg.**	**TDs**	**No.**	**Yds.**	**Avg.**	**Lg.**	**TDs**
1985	S.D.–Buff.	10	38	3.8	22	0	2	9	4.5	6	0
Totals		**10**	**38**	**3.8**	**22**	**0**	**2**	**9**	**4.5**	**6**	**0**

STROCK, Don MIAMI DOLPHINS
Position: Quarterback; **Birthdate:** 27.11.50
College: Virginia Tech; **Height:** 6–5; **Weight:** 220; **NFL Years:** 12

		PASSING						
Year	**Club**	**Att.**	**Comp.**	**Yds.**	**Lg.**	**TDs**	**Int.**	**Rat.**
1973	Miami			Did not play				
1974	Miami	0	0	0	0	0	0	00.0
1975	Miami	45	26	230	25	2	2	67.9
1976	Miami	47	21	359	53t	3	2	74.6
1977	Miami	4	2	12	9	0	1	16.7
1978	Miami	135	72	825	57	12	6	83.3
1979	Miami	100	56	830	53	6	6	78.3
1980	Miami	62	30	313	33	1	5	35.1
1981	Miami	130	79	901	52	6	8	71.1
1982	Miami	55	30	306	43	2	5	44.8
1983	Miami	52	34	403	47	4	1	106.5
1984	Miami	6	4	27	12	0	0	76.4
1985	Miami	9	7	141	67t	1	0	155.8
Totals		**645**	**361**	**4,347**	**67t**	**37**	**36**	**72.7**

SUHEY, Matt CHICAGO BEARS
Position: Running Back; **Birthdate:** 07.07.58
College: Penn State; **Height:** 5–11; **Weight:** 216; **NFL Years:** 6

		RUSHING					RECEIVING				
Year	Club	Att.	Yds.	Avg.	Lg.	TDs	No.	Yds.	Avg.	Lg.	TDs
1980	Chicago	22	45	2.0	10	0	7	60	8.6	21	0
1981	Chicago	150	521	3.5	26	3	33	168	5.1	15	0
1982	Chicago	70	206	2.9	15	3	36	333	9.3	45	0
1983	Chicago	149	681	4.6	39	4	49	429	8.8	52	1
1984	Chicago	124	424	3.4	21	4	42	312	7.4	23	2
1985	Chicago	115	471	4.1	17	1	33	295	8.9	35	1
Totals		**630**	**2,348**	**3.7**	**39**	**15**	**200**	**1,597**	**8.0**	**52**	**4**

SWEENEY, Calvin PITTSBURGH STEELERS
Position: Wide Receiver; **Birthdate:** 12.01.55
College: USC; **Height:** 6–2; **Weight:** 190; **NFL Years:** 6

		RECEIVING			
Year	Club	No.	Yds.	Avg.	Lg.	TDs
1979	Pittsburgh			Did not play		
1980	Pittsburgh	12	282	23.5	34	1
1981	Pittsburgh	2	53	26.5	32	0
1982	Pittsburgh	5	50	10.0	17	0
1983	Pittsburgh	39	577	14.8	42	5
1984	Pittsburgh	2	25	12.5	16	0
1985	Pittsburgh	16	234	14.6	69	0
Totals		**76**	**1,221**	**16.1**	**69**	**6**

TATUPU, Mosi NEW ENGLAND PATRIOTS
Position: Running Back; **Birthdate:** 26.04.55
College: USC; **Height:** 6–0; **Weight:** 227; **NFL Years:** 8

		RUSHING					RECEIVING				
Year	Club	Att.	Yds.	Avg.	Lg.	TDs	No.	Yds.	Avg.	Lg.	TDs
1978	New England	3	6	2.0	3	0	0	0	0.0	0	0
1979	New England	23	71	3.1	12	0	2	9	4.5	5	0
1980	New England	33	97	2.9	11	3	4	27	6.8	11	0

Year	Club	Att.	Yds.	Avg.	Lg.	TDs	No.	Yds.	Avg.	Lg.	TDs
1981	New England	38	201	5.3	43	2	12	132	11.0	41	1
1982	New England	30	168	5.6	26	0	0	0	0.0	0	0
1983	New England	106	578	5.5	55	4	10	97	9.7	17	1
1984	New England	133	553	4.2	20t	4	16	159	9.9	24	0
1985	New England	47	152	3.2	11	2	2	16	8.0	15	0
Totals		**413**	**1,826**	**4.4**	**55**	**15**	**46**	**440**	**9.6**	**41**	**2**

TEAL, Jimmy BUFFALO BILLS
Position: Wide Receiver; **Birthdate:** 18.08.62
College: Texas A&M; **Height:** 5–10; **Weight:** 170; **NFL Years:** 1

Year	Club		RECEIVING			
		No.	**Yds.**	**Avg.**	**Lg.**	**TDs**
1985	Buffalo	1	24	24.0	24	0
Totals		**1**	**24**	**24.0**	**24**	**0**

MATT SUHEY

CALVIN SWEENEY

THEISMANN, Joe WASHINGTON REDSKINS
Position: Quarterback; **Birthdate:** 09.09.49
College: Notre Dame; **Height:** 6–0; **Weight:** 198; **NFL Years:** 12

		PASSING						
Year	Club	Att.	Comp.	Yds.	Lg.	TDs	Int.	Rat.
1974	Washington	11	9	145	69	1	0	149.1
1975	Washington	22	10	96	30t	1	3	33.6
1976	Washington	163	79	1,036	44	8	10	59.9
1977	Washington	182	84	1,097	52	7	9	58.0
1978	Washington	390	187	2,593	63	13	18	61.6
1979	Washington	395	233	2,797	62	20	13	84.0
1980	Washington	454	262	2,962	54t	17	16	75.1
1981	Washington	496	293	3,568	79t	19	20	77.3
1982	Washington	252	161	2,033	78t	13	9	91.3
1983	Washington	459	276	3,714	84	29	11	97.0
1984	Washington	477	283	3,391	80t	24	13	86.6
1985	Washington	301	167	1,774	55	8	16	59.6
Totals		**3,602**	**2,044**	**25,206**	**84**	**160**	**138**	**77.4**

JOE THEISMANN

CALVIN THOMAS

THOMAS, Bob GREEN BAY PACKERS
Position: Placekicker; **Birthdate:** 07.08.52
College: Notre Dame; **Height:** 5–10; **Weight:** 177; **NFL Years:** 10

		SCORING					
Year	**Club**	**EPA**	**EPM**	**FGA**	**FGM**	**Lg.**	**Pts.**
1975	Chicago	22	18	23	13	55	57
1976	Chicago	30	27	25	12	47	63
1977	Chicago	30	27	27	14	47	69
1978	Chicago	28	26	22	17	44	77
1979	Chicago	37	34	27	16	44	82
1980	Chicago	37	35	18	13	44	74
1981	Chicago	3	2	3	2	37	8
1982	Det.-Chi.	9	9	12	10	46	39
1983	Chicago	38	35	25	14	50	77
1984	Chicago	37	35	28	22	52	101
1985	San Diego	55	51	28	18	46	105
Totals		**326**	**299**	**238**	**151**	**55**	**752**

THOMAS, Calvin CHICAGO BEARS
Position: Running Back; **Birthdate:** 07.01.60
College: Illinois; **Height:** 5–11; **Weight:** 245; **NFL Years:** 4

		RUSHING					RECEIVING				
Year	**Club**	**Att.**	**Yds.**	**Avg.**	**Lg.**	**TDs**	**No.**	**Yds.**	**Avg.**	**Lg.**	**TDs**
1982	Chicago	5	4	0.8	3	0	0	0	0.0	0	0
1983	Chicago	8	25	3.1	9	0	2	13	6.5	7	0
1984	Chicago	40	186	4.7	37	1	9	39	4.3	9	0
1985	Chicago	31	125	4.0	17	4	5	45	9.0	15	0
Totals		**84**	**340**	**4.0**	**37**	**5**	**16**	**97**	**6.1**	**15**	**0**

LEONARD THOMPSON

WEEGIE THOMPSON

THOMPSON, Leonard DETROIT LIONS
Position: Wide Receiver; **Birthdate:** 28.07.52
College: Oklahoma State; **Height:** 5–11; **Weight:** 192; **NFL Years:** 11

		RECEIVING				
Year	Club	No.	Yds.	Avg.	Lg.	TDs
1975	Detroit	0	0	0.0	0	0
1976	Detroit	3	52	17.3	21	0
1977	Detroit	7	42	6.0	18	0
1978	Detroit	10	167	16.7	45t	4
1979	Detroit	24	451	18.8	82	2
1980	Detroit	19	511	26.9	79t	3
1981	Detroit	30	550	18.3	94t	3
1982	Detroit	17	328	19.3	70t	4
1983	Detroit	41	752	18.3	80t	3
1984	Detroit	50	773	15.5	66t	6
1985	Detroit	51	736	14.4	48	5
Totals		**252**	**4,362**	**17.3**	**94t**	**30**

THOMPSON, Weegie PITTSBURGH STEELERS
Position: Wide Receiver; **Birthdate:** 21.03.61
College: Florida State; **Height:** 6–6; **Weight:** 211; **NFL Years:** 2

		RECEIVING				
Year	**Club**	**No.**	**Yds.**	**Avg.**	**Lg.**	**TDs**
1984	Pittsburgh	17	291	17.1	59	3
1985	Pittsburgh	8	138	17.3	42	1
Totals		**25**	**429**	**17.2**	**59**	**4**

TICE, John NEW ORLEANS SAINTS
Position: Tight End; **Birthdate:** 22.06.60
College: Maryland; **Height:** 6–5; **Weight:** 243; **NFL Years:** 3

		RECEIVING				
Year	**Club**	**No.**	**Yds.**	**Avg.**	**Lg.**	**TDs**
1983	New Orleans	7	33	4.7	12t	1
1984	New Orleans	6	55	9.2	17	1
1985	New Orleans	24	266	11.1	39t	2
Totals		**37**	**354**	**9.6**	**39t**	**4**

TICE, Mike SEATTLE SEAHAWKS
Position: Tight End; **Birthdate:** 02.02.59
College: Maryland; **Height:** 6–7; **Weight:** 250; **NFL Years:** 5

		RECEIVING				
Year	**Club**	**No.**	**Yds.**	**Avg.**	**Lg.**	**TDs**
1981	Seattle	5	47	9.4	14	0
1982	Seattle	9	46	5.1	12	0
1983	Seattle	0	0	0.0	0	0
1984	Seattle	8	90	11.3	30	3
1985	Seattle	2	13	6.5	7	0
Totals		**24**	**196**	**8.2**	**30**	**3**

TILLEY, Pat ST. LOUIS CARDINALS
Position: Wide Receiver; **Birthdate:** 15.02.53
College: Louisiana Tech; **Height:** 5–10; **Weight:** 178; **NFL Years:** 10

		RECEIVING				
Year	**Club**	**No.**	**Yds.**	**Avg.**	**Lg.**	**TDs**
1976	St. Louis	26	407	15.7	45	1
1977	St. Louis	5	64	12.8	31	0
1978	St. Louis	62	900	14.5	43	3
1979	St. Louis	57	938	16.5	51t	6
1980	St. Louis	68	966	14.2	60t	6
1981	St. Louis	66	1,040	15.8	75	3
1982	St. Louis	36	465	12.9	34	2
1983	St. Louis	44	690	15.7	71t	5
1984	St. Louis	52	758	14.6	42	5
1985	St. Louis	49	726	14.8	46t	6
Totals		**465**	**6,954**	**15.0**	**75**	**37**

TODD, Richard NEW ORLEANS SAINTS
Position: Quarterback; **Birthdate:** 19.11.53
College: Alabama; **Height:** 6–2; **Weight:** 212; **NFL Years:** 10

		PASSING						
Year	**Club**	**Att.**	**Comp.**	**Yds.**	**Lg.**	**TDs**	**Int.**	**Rat.**
1976	N.Y. Jets	162	65	870	44t	3	12	33.4
1977	N.Y. Jets	265	133	1,863	87t	11	17	60.6
1978	N.Y. Jets	107	60	849	49	6	10	61.8
1979	N.Y. Jets	334	171	2,660	72t	16	22	66.4
1980	N.Y. Jets	479	264	3,329	55	17	30	62.4
1981	N.Y. Jets	497	279	3,231	49	25	13	81.8
1982	N.Y. Jets	261	153	1,961	56t	14	8	87.3
1983	N.Y. Jets	518	308	3,478	64t	18	26	70.3
1984	New Orleans	312	161	2,178	74	11	19	60.6
1985	New Orleans	32	16	191	56t	3	4	60.3
Totals		**2,967**	**1,610**	**20,610**	**87t**	**124**	**161**	**67.6**

TOON, Al NEW YORK JETS
Position: Wide Receiver; **Birthdate:** 30.04.63
College: Wisconsin; **Height:** 6–4; **Weight:** 200; **NFL Years:** 1

		RECEIVING				
Year	**Club**	**No.**	**Yds.**	**Avg.**	**Lg.**	**TDs**
1985	N.Y. Jets	46	662	14.4	78t	3
Totals		**46**	**662**	**14.4**	**78t**	**3**

TOWNSELL, JoJo NEW YORK JETS
Position: Wide Receiver; **Birthdate:** 04.11.60
College: UCLA; **Height:** 5–9; **Weight:** 180; **NFL Years:** 1

		RECEIVING				
Year	**Club**	**No.**	**Yds.**	**Avg.**	**Lg.**	**TDs**
1985	N.Y. Jets	12	187	15.6	36	0
Totals		**12**	**187**	**15.6**	**36**	**0**

PAT TILLEY

RICHARD TODD

TURNER, Daryl SEATTLE SEAHAWKS
Position: Wide Receiver; **Birthdate:** 15.12.61
College: Michigan State; **Height:** 6–3; **Weight:** 198; **NFL Years:** 2

		RECEIVING				
Year	Club	No.	Yds.	Avg.	Lg.	TDs
1984	Seattle	35	715	20.4	80t	10
1985	Seattle	34	670	19.7	54	13
Totals		**69**	**1,385**	**20.1**	**80t**	**23**

TYLER, Wendell SAN FRANCISCO 49ers
Position: Running Back; **Birthdate:** 20.05.55
College: UCLA; **Height:** 5–10; **Weight:** 200; **NFL Years:** 9

		RUSHING					RECEIVING				
Year	Club	Att.	Yds.	Avg.	Lg.	TDs	No.	Yds.	Avg.	Lg.	TDs
1977	L.A. Rams	61	317	5.2	44t	3	1	3	3.0	3	0
1978	L.A. Rams	14	45	3.2	18	0	2	17	8.5	16	0
1979	L.A. Rams	218	1,109	5.1	63t	9	32	308	9.6	71t	1
1980	L.A. Rams	30	157	5.2	17	0	2	8	4.0	5	0
1981	L.A. Rams	260	1,074	4.1	69t	12	45	436	9.7	67t	5
1982	L.A. Rams	137	564	4.1	54	9	38	375	9.9	40	4
1983	San Francisco	176	856	4.9	39	4	34	285	8.4	26	2
1984	San Francisco	246	1,262	5.1	40	7	28	230	8.2	26t	2
1985	San Francisco	171	867	5.1	30	6	20	154	7.7	16	2
Totals		**1,313**	**6,251**	**4.8**	**69t**	**50**	**202**	**1,816**	**9.0**	**71t**	**16**

VERSER, David TAMPA BAY BUCCANEERS
Position: Wide Receiver; **Birthdate:** 01.03.58
College: Kansas; **Height:** 6–1; **Weight:** 202; **NFL Years:** 4

		RECEIVING				
Year	Club	No.	Yds.	Avg.	Lg.	TDs
1981	Cincinnati	6	161	26.8	73t	2
1982	Cincinnati	4	98	24.5	56t	1
1983	Cincinnati	7	82	11.7	22	0
1984	Cincinnati	6	113	18.8	28	0
1985	Tampa Bay	0	0	0.0	0	0
Totals		**23**	**454**	**19.7**	**73t**	**3**

DARYL TURNER

WENDELL TYLER

VIGORITO, Tommy MIAMI DOLPHINS
Position: Wide Receiver; **Birthdate:** 23.10.59
College: Virginia; **Height:** 5–10; **Weight:** 190; **NFL Years:** 3

				RECEIVING		
Year	Club	No.	Yds.	Avg.	Lg.	TDs
1981	Miami	33	237	7.2	31t	2
1982	Miami	24	186	7.8	26	0
1983	Miami	1	7	7.0	7	0
1984	Miami			Did not play		
1985	Miami	1	9	9.0	9	0
Totals		**59**	**439**	**7.4**	**31t**	**2**

WALKER, Byron SEATTLE SEAHAWKS
Position: Wide Receiver; **Birthdate:** 28.07.60
College: Citadel; **Height:** 6–4; **Weight:** 190; **NFL Years:** 4

				RECEIVING		
Year	Club	No.	Yds.	Avg.	Lg.	TDs
1982	Seattle	10	156	15.6	40t	2
1983	Seattle	12	248	20.7	50t	2
1984	Seattle	13	236	18.2	41	1
1985	Seattle	19	285	15.0	28t	2
Totals		**54**	**925**	**17.1**	**50t**	**7**

187

WESLEY WALKER

CURT WARNER

WALKER, Rick WASHINGTON REDSKINS
Position: Tight End; **Birthdate:** 28.05.55
College: UCLA; **Height:** 6–4; **Weight:** 235; **NFL Years:** 9

		RECEIVING				
Year	Club	No.	Yds.	Avg.	Lg.	TDs
1977	Cincinnati	1	13	13.0	13	0
1978	Cincinnati	12	126	10.5	28	2
1979	Cincinnati	1	14	14.0	14t	1
1980	Washington	10	88	8.8	15t	1
1981	Washington	11	112	10.2	24	1
1982	Washington	12	92	7.7	25t	1
1983	Washington	17	168	9.9	29	2
1984	Washington	5	52	10.4	19	1
1985	Washington	1	8	8.0	8	0
Totals		**70**	**673**	**9.6**	**29**	**9**

WALKER, Wesley NEW YORK JETS
Position: Wide Receiver; **Birthdate:** 26.05.55
College: California; **Height:** 6–0; **Weight:** 182; **NFL Years:** 9

		RECEIVING				
Year	Club	No.	Yds.	Avg.	Lg.	TDs
1977	N.Y. Jets	35	740	21.1	87t	3
1978	N.Y. Jets	48	1,169	24.4	77t	8
1979	N.Y. Jets	23	569	24.7	71t	5
1980	N.Y. Jets	18	376	20.9	47	1
1981	N.Y. Jets	47	770	16.4	49	9
1982	N.Y. Jets	39	620	15.9	56t	6
1983	N.Y. Jets	61	868	14.2	64t	7
1984	N.Y. Jets	41	623	15.2	44t	7
1985	N.Y. Jets	34	725	21.3	96t	5
Totals		**346**	**6,460**	**18.7**	**96t**	**51**

WALLS, Herkie HOUSTON OILERS
Position: Wide Receiver; **Birthdate:** 18.07.61
College: Texas; **Height:** 5–8; **Weight:** 160; **NFL Years:** 3

		RECEIVING				
Year	Club	No.	Yds.	Avg.	Lg.	TDs
1983	Houston	12	276	23.0	48	1
1984	Houston	18	291	16.2	76	1
1985	Houston	1	7	7.0	7	0
Totals		**31**	**574**	**18.5**	**76**	**2**

WARNER, Curt SEATTLE SEAHAWKS
Position: Running Back; **Birthdate:** 18.03.61
College: Penn State; **Height:** 5–11; **Weight:** 205; **NFL Years:** 2

		RUSHING					RECEIVING				
Year	Club	Att.	Yds.	Avg.	Lg.	TDs	No.	Yds.	Avg.	Lg.	TDs
1983	Seattle	335	1,449	4.3	60	13	42	325	7.7	28	1
1984	Seattle	10	40	4.0	9	0	1	19	19.0	19	0
1985	Seattle	291	1,094	3.8	38	8	47	307	6.5	27t	1
Totals		**636**	**2,583**	**4.1**	**60**	**21**	**90**	**651**	**7.2**	**28**	**2**

189

WARREN, Don WASHINGTON REDSKINS
Position: Tight End; **Birthdate:** 05.05.56
College: San Diego State; **Height:** 6–4; **Weight:** 242; **NFL Years:** 7

		RECEIVING				
Year	Club	No.	Yds.	Avg.	Lg.	TDs
1979	Washington	26	303	11.7	23	0
1980	Washington	31	323	10.4	35	0
1981	Washington	29	335	11.6	32	1
1982	Washington	27	310	11.5	29	0
1983	Washington	20	225	11.3	33	2
1984	Washington	18	192	10.7	26	0
1985	Washington	15	163	10.9	19	1
Totals		**166**	**1,851**	**11.2**	**35**	**4**

WASHINGTON, Joe
Position: Running Back; **Birthdate:** 24.09.53
College: Oklahoma; **Height:** 5–10; **Weight:** 179; **NFL Years:** 9

		RUSHING					RECEIVING				
Year	Club	Att.	Yds.	Avg.	Lg.	TDs	No.	Yds.	Avg.	Lg.	TDs
1976	San Diego					Did not play					
1977	San Diego	62	217	3.5	19	0	31	244	7.9	29	0

DON WARREN

STEVE WATSON

Year	Club	Att.	Yds.	Avg.	Lg.	TDs	No.	Yds.	Avg.	Lg.	TDs
1978	Baltimore	240	956	4.0	29	0	45	377	8.4	33	1
1979	Baltimore	242	884	3.7	26	4	82	750	9.1	43t	3
1980	Baltimore	144	502	3.5	17	1	51	494	9.7	33	3
1981	Washington	210	916	4.4	32	4	70	558	8.0	32	3
1982	Washington	44	190	4.3	40	1	19	134	7.1	17	1
1983	Washington	145	772	5.3	41	0	47	454	9.7	67	6
1984	Washington	56	192	3.4	12	1	13	74	5.7	12	0
1985	Atlanta	52	210	4.0	14	1	37	328	8.9	34	1
Totals		**1,195**	**4,839**	**4.0**	**41**	**12**	**395**	**3,413**	**8.6**	**67**	**18**

WATSON, Steve DENVER BRONCOS
Position: Wide Receiver; **Birthdate:** 28.05.57
College: Temple; **Height:** 6–4; **Weight:** 195; **NFL Years:** 7

		RECEIVING			
Year	Club	No.	Yds.	Avg.	Lg.	TDs
1979	Denver	6	83	13.8	22	0
1980	Denver	6	146	24.3	52	0
1981	Denver	60	1,244	20.7	95t	13
1982	Denver	36	555	15.4	41	2
1983	Denver	59	1,133	19.2	78t	5
1984	Denver	69	1,170	17.0	73	7
1985	Denver	61	915	15.0	60	5
Totals		**297**	**5,246**	**17.7**	**95t**	**32**

WEATHERS, Clarence CLEVELAND BROWNS
Position: Wide Receiver; **Birthdate:** 10.01.62
College: Delaware State; **Height:** 5–9; **Weight:** 170; **NFL Years:** 3

		RECEIVING			
Year	Club	No.	Yds.	Avg.	Lg.	TDs
1983	New England	19	379	19.9	58t	3
1984	New England	8	115	14.4	29	2
1985	Cleveland	16	449	28.1	72t	3
Totals		**43**	**943**	**21.9**	**72t**	**8**

RAY WERSCHING

CHARLES WHITE

WEATHERS, Robert NEW ENGLAND PATRIOTS
Position: Running Back; **Birthdate:** 13.09.60
College: Arizona State; **Height:** 6–2; **Weight:** 222; **NFL Years:** 4

Year	Club	RUSHING					RECEIVING				
		Att.	Yds.	Avg.	Lg.	TDs	No.	Yds.	Avg.	Lg.	TDs
1982	New England	24	83	3.5	18	1	3	24	8.0	22	0
1983	New England	73	418	5.7	77	1	23	212	9.2	19	0
1984	New England	0	0	0.0	0	0	0	0	0.0	0	0
1985	New England	41	174	4.2	42t	1	2	18	9.0	13	0
Totals		**138**	**675**	**4.9**	**77**	**3**	**28**	**254**	**9.1**	**22**	**0**

WERSCHING, Ray SAN FRANCISCO 49ers
Position: Placekicker; **Birthdate:** 21.08.50
College: California; **Height:** 5–11; **Weight:** 215; **NFL Years:** 13

Year	Club	SCORING					
		EPA	EPM	FGA	FGM	Lg.	Pts.
1973	San Diego	15	13	25	11	39	46
1974	San Diego	0	0	11	5	42	15

Year	Club	EPA	EPM	FGA	FGM	Lg.	Pts.
1975	San Diego	21	20	24	12	45	56
1976	San Diego	16	14	8	4	45	26
1977	San Francisco	23	23	17	10	50	53
1978	San Francisco	25	24	23	15	45	69
1979	San Francisco	35	32	24	20	47	92
1980	San Francisco	39	33	19	15	47	78
1981	San Francisco	30	30	23	17	48	81
1982	San Francisco	25	23	17	12	45	59
1983	San Francisco	51	51	30	25	52	126
1984	San Francisco	56	56	35	25	53	131
1985	San Francisco	53	52	21	13	45	91
Totals		**389**	**371**	**277**	**184**	**53**	**923**

WEST, Ed GREEN BAY PACKERS
Position: Tight End; **Birthdate:** 02.08.61
College: Auburn; **Height:** 6–1; **Weight:** 242; **NFL Years:** 2

		RECEIVING				
Year	Club	No.	Yds.	Avg.	Lg.	TDs
1984	Green Bay	6	54	9.0	29t	4
1985	Green Bay	8	95	11.9	30	1
Totals		**14**	**149**	**10.6**	**30**	**5**

WHITE, Charles LOS ANGELES RAMS
Position: Running Back; **Birthdate:** 22.01.58
College: USC; **Height:** 5–10; **Weight:** 190; **NFL Years:** 5

		RUSHING					RECEIVING				
Year	Club	Att.	Yds.	Avg.	Lg.	TDs	No.	Yds.	Avg.	Lg.	TDs
1980	Cleveland	86	279	3.2	16	5	17	153	9.0	31t	1
1981	Cleveland	97	342	3.5	26	1	27	219	8.1	21	0
1982	Cleveland	69	259	3.8	18t	3	34	283	8.3	36	0
1983	Cleveland					Did not play					
1984	Cleveland	24	62	2.6	8	0	5	29	5.8	17	0
1985	L.A. Rams	70	310	4.4	32	3	1	12	12.0	12	0
Totals		**346**	**1,252**	**3.6**	**32**	**12**	**84**	**696**	**8.3**	**36**	**1**

193

WHITE, Danny DALLAS COWBOYS
Position: Quarterback; **Birthdate:** 09.02.52
College: Arizona State; **Height:** 6–3; **Weight:** 196; **NFL Years:** 10

		PASSING						
Year	**Club**	**Att.**	**Comp.**	**Yds.**	**Lg.**	**TDs**	**Int.**	**Rat.**
1976	Dallas	20	13	213	56	2	2	94.4
1977	Dallas	10	4	35	12	0	1	10.4
1978	Dallas	34	20	215	35	0	1	65.3
1979	Dallas	39	19	267	45	1	2	58.6
1980	Dallas	436	260	3,287	58t	28	25	80.8
1981	Dallas	391	223	3,098	73t	22	13	87.5
1982	Dallas	247	156	2,079	49	16	12	91.1
1983	Dallas	533	334	3,980	80t	29	23	85.6
1984	Dallas	233	126	1,580	66t	11	11	71.5
1985	Dallas	450	267	3,157	56t	21	17	80.6
Totals		**2,393**	**1,422**	**17,911**	**80t**	**130**	**107**	**82.3**

WHITE, Sammy MINNESOTA VIKINGS
Position: Wide Receiver; **Birthdate:** 16.03.54
College: Grambling State; **Height:** 5–11; **Weight:** 200; **NFL Years:** 10

		RECEIVING				
Year	**Club**	**No.**	**Yds.**	**Avg.**	**Lg.**	**TDs**
1976	Minnesota	51	906	17 8	56t	10
1977	Minnesota	41	760	18.5	69t	9
1978	Minnesota	53	741	14.0	33t	9
1979	Minnesota	42	715	17 0	55t	4
1980	Minnesota	53	887	16.7	50	5
1981	Minnesota	66	1,001	15.2	53	3
1982	Minnesota	29	503	17 3	65	5
1983	Minnesota	29	412	14.2	43t	4
1984	Minnesota	21	399	19.0	47	1
1985	Minnesota	8	76	9.5	15	0
Totals		**393**	**6,400**	**16.3**	**69t**	**50**

DANNY WHITE

JAMES WILDER

WILDER, James TAMPA BAY BUCCANEERS
Position: Running Back; **Birthdate:** 12.05.58
College: Missouri; **Height:** 6–3; **Weight:** 225; **NFL Years:** 5

		RUSHING					RECEIVING				
Year	Club	Att.	Yds.	Avg.	Lg.	TDs	No.	Yds.	Avg.	Lg.	TDs
1981	Tampa Bay	107	370	3.5	23t	4	48	507	10.6	38	1
1982	Tampa Bay	83	324	3.9	47	3	53	466	8.8	32	1
1983	Tampa Bay	161	640	4.0	75t	4	57	380	6.7	31	2
1984	Tampa Bay	407	1,544	3.8	37	13	85	685	8.1	50	0
1985	Tampa Bay	365	1,300	3.6	28	10	53	341	6.4	20	0
Totals		**1,123**	**4,178**	**3.7**	**75t**	**34**	**296**	**2,379**	**8.0**	**50**	**4**

WILLHITE, Gerald DENVER BRONCOS
Position: Running Back; **Birthdate:** 30.05.59
College: San Jose State; **Height:** 5–10; **Weight:** 200; **NFL Years:** 4

		RUSHING					RECEIVING				
Year	Club	Att.	Yds.	Avg.	Lg.	TDs	No.	Yds.	Avg.	Lg.	TDs
1982	Denver	70	347	5.0	23	2	26	227	8.7	27	0
1983	Denver	43	188	4.4	24t	3	14	153	10.9	26t	1
1984	Denver	77	371	4.8	52	2	27	298	11.0	63	0
1985	Denver	66	237	3.6	14	3	35	297	8.5	21	1
Totals		**256**	**1,143**	**4.5**	**52**	**10**	**102**	**975**	**9.6**	**63**	**2**

WILLIAMS, Byron NEW YORK GIANTS
Position: Wide Receiver; **Birthdate:** 31.10.60
College: Texas-Arlington; **Height:** 6–2; **Weight:** 183; **NFL Years:** 3

Year	Club	No.	Yds.	Avg.	Lg.	TDs
				RECEIVING		
1983	Phil.–N.Y.G.	20	346	17 3	43t	1
1984	N.Y. Giants	24	471	19.6	65t	2
1985	N.Y. Giants	15	280	18.7	45	0
Totals		**59**	**1,097**	**18.6**	**65t**	**3**

WILLIAMS, Derwin NEW ENGLAND PATRIOTS
Position: Wide Receiver; **Birthdate:** 06.05.61
College: New Mexico; **Height:** 6–0; **Weight:** 170; **NFL Years:** 1

Year	Club	No.	Yds.	Avg.	Lg.	TDs
				RECEIVING		
1984	New England			Did not play		

JAMIE WILLIAMS   DOKIE WILLIAMS

Year	Club	No.	Yds.	Avg.	Lg.	TDs
1985	New England	9	163	18.1	30	0
Totals		**9**	**163**	**18.1**	**30**	**0**

WILLIAMS, Dokie LOS ANGELES RAIDERS
Position: Wide Receiver; **Birthdate:** 25.08.60
College: UCLA; **Height:** 5–11; **Weight:** 180; **NFL Years:** 3

				RECEIVING		
Year	Club	No.	Yds.	Avg.	Lg.	TDs
1983	L.A. Raiders	14	259	18.5	50t	3
1984	L.A. Raiders	22	509	23.1	75t	4
1985	L.A. Raiders	48	925	19.3	55	5
Totals		**84**	**1,693**	**20.2**	**75t**	**12**

WILLIAMS, Jamie HOUSTON OILERS
Position: Tight End; **Birthdate:** 25.02.60
College: Nebraska; **Height:** 6–4; **Weight:** 232; **NFL Years:** 3

				RECEIVING		
Year	Club	No.	Yds.	Avg.	Lg.	TDs
1983	St. Louis	0	0	0.0	0	0
1984	Houston	41	545	13.3	32	3
1985	Houston	39	444	11.4	29	1
Totals		**80**	**989**	**12.4**	**32**	**4**

WILLIAMS, Oliver INDIANAPOLIS COLTS
Position: Wide Receiver; **Birthdate:** 17 10.60
College: Illinois; **Height:** 6–3; **Weight:** 191; **NFL Years:** 1

				RECEIVING		
Year	Club	No.	Yds.	Avg.	Lg.	TDs
1985	Indianapolis	9	175	19.4	30	1
Totals		**9**	**175**	**19.4**	**30**	**1**

WILSON, Dave NEW ORLEANS SAINTS
Position: Quarterback; **Birthdate:** 27.04.59
College: Illinois; **Height:** 6–3; **Weight:** 211; **NFL Years:** 4

| | | PASSING | | | | | | |
Year	Club	Att.	Comp.	Yds.	Lg.	TDs	Int.	Rat.
1981	New Orleans	159	82	1,058	50	1	11	46.1
1982	New Orleans			Did not play				
1983	New Orleans	112	66	770	42	5	7	68.7
1984	New Orleans	93	51	647	54t	7	4	83.9
1985	New Orleans	293	145	1,843	50	11	15	60.7
Totals		**657**	**344**	**4,318**	**54t**	**24**	**37**	**61.8**

WILSON, Marc LOS ANGELES RAIDERS
Position: Quarterback; **Birthdate:** 15.02.57
College: Brigham Young; **Height:** 6–6; **Weight:** 205; **NFL Years:** 6

| | | PASSING | | | | | | |
Year	Club	Att.	Comp.	Yds.	Lg.	TDs	Int.	Rat.
1980	Oakland	5	3	31	12	0	0	77.9
1981	Oakland	366	173	2,311	66t	14	19	58.8
1982	L.A. Raiders	2	1	4	4	0	0	56.3
1983	L.A. Raiders	117	67	864	50t	8	6	82.0
1984	L.A. Raiders	282	153	2,151	92	15	17	71.7
1985	L.A. Raiders	388	193	2,608	59	16	21	62.7
Totals		**1,160**	**590**	**7,969**	**92**	**53**	**63**	**65.7**

WILSON, Mike SAN FRANCISCO 49ers
Position: Wide Receiver; **Birthdate:** 19.12.58
College: Washington State; **Height:** 6–3; **Weight:** 215; **NFL Years:** 5

| | | RECEIVING | | | | |
Year	Club	No.	Yds.	Avg.	Lg.	TDs
1981	San Francisco	9	125	13.9	27t	1
1982	San Francisco	6	80	13.3	27	1
1983	San Francisco	30	433	14.4	49	0
1984	San Francisco	17	245	14.4	44	1
1985	San Francisco	10	165	16.5	52t	2
Totals		**72**	**1,048**	**14.6**	**52t**	**5**

WILSON, Wade MINNESOTA VIKINGS
Position: Quarterback; **Birthdate:** 01.02.59
College: East Texas State; **Height:** 6–3; **Weight:** 210; **NFL Years:** 5

		PASSING						
Year	**Club**	**Att.**	**Comp.**	**Yds.**	**Lg.**	**TDs**	**Int.**	**Rat.**
1981	Minnesota	13	6	48	22	0	2	16.4
1982	Minnesota	0	0	0	0	0	0	00.0
1983	Minnesota	28	16	124	36	1	2	50.3
1984	Minnesota	195	102	1,019	38	5	11	52.5
1985	Minnesota	60	33	404	42t	3	3	71.8
Totals		**296**	**157**	**1,595**	**42t**	**9**	**18**	**53.5**

MARC WILSON

MIKE WILSON

WILSON, Wayne NEW ORLEANS SAINTS
Position: Running Back; **Birthdate:** 04.09.57
College: Shepherd; **Height:** 6–3; **Weight:** 220; **NFL Years:** 7

		RUSHING					RECEIVING				
Year	Club	Att.	Yds.	Avg.	Lg.	TDs	No.	Yds.	Avg.	Lg.	TDs
1979	New Orleans	5	26	5.2	16	0	0	0	0.0	0	0
1980	New Orleans	63	188	3.0	15	1	31	241	7.8	42	1
1981	New Orleans	44	137	3.1	13	1	31	384	12.4	55	4
1982	New Orleans	103	413	4.0	20	3	25	175	7.0	34	2
1983	New Orleans	199	787	4.0	29	9	20	178	8.9	24	2
1984	New Orleans	74	261	3.5	36	1	33	314	9.5	34t	3
1985	New Orleans	168	645	3.8	41t	1	38	228	6.0	21	2
Totals		**656**	**2,457**	**3.7**	**41t**	**16**	**178**	**1,520**	**8.5**	**55**	**14**

SAMMY WINDER

KELLEN WINSLOW

WINDER, Sammy DENVER BRONCOS
Position: Running Back; **Birthdate:** 15.07.59
College: So. Mississippi; **Height:** 5–11; **Weight:** 203; **NFL Years:** 4

		RUSHING					RECEIVING				
Year	Club	Att.	Yds.	Avg.	Lg.	TDs	No.	Yds.	Avg.	Lg.	TDs
1982	Denver	67	259	3.9	18	1	11	83	7.5	22	0
1983	Denver	196	757	3.9	52	3	23	150	6.5	17	0
1984	Denver	296	1,153	3.9	24	4	44	288	6.5	21	2
1985	Denver	199	714	3.6	42	8	31	197	6.4	24	0
Totals		**758**	**2,883**	**3.8**	**52**	**16**	**109**	**718**	**6.6**	**24**	**2**

WINSLOW, Kellen SAN DIEGO CHARGERS
Position: Tight End; **Birthdate:** 05.11.57
College: Missouri; **Height:** 6–5; **Weight:** 242; **NFL Years:** 7

		RECEIVING			
Year	Club	No.	Yds.	Avg.	Lg.	TDs
1979	San Diego	25	255	10.2	30	2
1980	San Diego	89	1,290	14.5	65	9
1981	San Diego	88	1,075	12.2	67t	10
1982	San Diego	54	721	13.4	40	6
1983	San Diego	88	1,172	13.3	46	8
1984	San Diego	55	663	12.1	33	2
1985	San Diego	25	318	12.7	26	0
Totals		**424**	**5,494**	**13.0**	**67t**	**37**

WITTE, Mark TAMPA BAY BUCCANEERS
Position: Tight End; **Birthdate:** 03.12.59
College: North Texas State; **Height:** 6–3; **Weight:** 240; **NFL Years:** 3

		RECEIVING			
Year	Club	No.	Yds.	Avg.	Lg.	TDs
1983	Tampa Bay	2	15	7 5	10	0
1984	Tampa Bay	0	0	0.0	0	0
1985	Tampa Bay	3	28	9.3	13	0
Totals		**5**	**43**	**8.6**	**13**	**0**

RON WOLFLEY

GEORGE WONSLEY

WOLFLEY, Ron ST. LOUIS CARDINALS
Position: Running Back; **Birthdate:** 14.10.62
College: West Virginia; **Height:** 6–0; **Weight:** 222; **NFL Years:** 1

		RUSHING					RECEIVING				
Year	Club	Att.	Yds.	Avg.	Lg.	TDs	No.	Yds.	Avg.	Lg.	TDs
1985	St. Louis	24	64	2.7	11	0	2	18	9.0	17	0
Totals		**24**	**64**	**2.7**	**11**	**0**	**2**	**18**	**9.0**	**17**	**0**

WONSLEY, George INDIANAPOLIS COLTS
Position: Running Back; **Birthdate:** 23.11.60
College: Mississippi State; **Height:** 6–0; **Weight:** 217; **NFL Years:** 2

		RUSHING					RECEIVING				
Year	Club	Att.	Yds.	Avg.	Lg.	TDs	No.	Yds.	Avg.	Lg.	TDs
1984	Indianapolis	37	111	3.0	13	0	9	47	5.2	17	0
1985	Indianapolis	138	716	5.2	36	6	30	257	8.6	26	0
Totals		**175**	**827**	**4.7**	**36**	**6**	**39**	**304**	**7.8**	**26**	**0**

WONSLEY, Otis WASHINGTON REDSKINS
Position: Running Back; **Birthdate:** 13.08.57
College: Alcorn State; **Height:** 5–10; **Weight:** 214; **NFL Years:** 5

		RUSHING					RECEIVING				
Year	Club	Att.	Yds.	Avg.	Lg.	TDs	No.	Yds.	Avg.	Lg.	TDs
1981	Washington	3	11	3.7	7	0	1	5	5.0	5	0
1982	Washington	11	36	3.3	7	0	1	1	1.0	1t	1
1983	Washington	25	88	3.5	9	0	0	0	0.0	0	0
1984	Washington	18	38	2.1	7	4	0	0	0.0	0	0
1985	Washington	4	8	2.0	5	0	0	0	0.0	0	0
Totals		**61**	**181**	**3.0**	**9**	**4**	**2**	**6**	**3.0**	**5**	**1**

WOODLEY, David PITTSBURGH STEELERS
Position: Quarterback; **Birthdate:** 25.10.58
College: Louisiana State; **Height:** 6–2; **Weight:** 210; **NFL Years:** 6

		PASSING						
Year	Club	Att.	Comp.	Yds.	Lg.	TDs	Int.	Rat.
1980	Miami	327	176	1,850	61	14	17	63.2
1981	Miami	366	191	2,470	69t	12	13	69.7
1982	Miami	179	98	1,080	46	5	8	63.4
1983	Miami	89	43	528	64t	3	4	59.6
1984	Pittsburgh	156	85	1,273	80t	8	7	79.9
1985	Pittsburgh	183	94	1,357	69	6	14	54.8
Totals		**1,300**	**687**	**8,558**	**80t**	**48**	**63**	**65.7**

WOODRUFF, Tony PHILADELPHIA EAGLES
Position: Wide Receiver; **Birthdate:** 12.11.58
College: Fresno State; **Height:** 6–0; **Weight:** 185; **NFL Years:** 3

		RECEIVING				
Year	Club	No.	Yds.	Avg.	Lg.	TDs
1982	Philadelphia	0	0	0.0	0	0
1983	Philadelphia	6	70	11.7	29t	2
1984	Philadelphia	30	484	16.1	38	3
1985	Philadelphia			Did not play		
Totals		**36**	**554**	**15.4**	**38**	**5**

203

WOOLFOLK, Butch HOUSTON OILERS
Position: Running Back; **Birthdate:** 01.03.60
College: Michigan; **Height:** 6–1; **Weight:** 212; **NFL Years:** 4

		RUSHING					RECEIVING				
Year	Club	Att.	Yds.	Avg.	Lg.	TDs	No.	Yds.	Avg.	Lg.	TDs
1982	N.Y. Giants	112	439	3.9	18	2	23	224	9.7	40t	2
1983	N.Y. Giants	246	857	3.5	22	4	28	368	13.1	44	0
1984	N.Y. Giants	40	92	2.3	17	1	9	53	5.9	13	0
1985	Houston	103	392	3.8	43	1	80	814	10.2	80t	4
Totals		**501**	**1,780**	**3.6**	**43**	**8**	**140**	**1,459**	**10.4**	**80t**	**6**

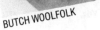

BUTCH WOOLFOLK

TIM WRIGHTMAN

WRIGHT, Jim DENVER BRONCOS
Position: Tight End; **Birthdate:** 01.09.56
College: Texas Christian; **Height:** 6–3; **Weight:** 240; **NFL Years:** 6

		RECEIVING				
Year	Club	No.	Yds.	Avg.	Lg.	TDs
1978	Atlanta	2	26	13.0	18	0
1979	Atlanta			Did not play		
1980	Denver	0	0	0.0	0	0
1981	Denver	3	22	7 3	14	1
1982	Denver	9	120	13.3	39	1
1983	Denver	13	134	10.3	23	0
1984	Denver	11	118	10.7	21	1
1985	Denver	28	246	8.8	30	1
Totals		**66**	**666**	**10.1**	**39**	**4**

WRIGHT, Randy GREEN BAY PACKERS
Position: Quarterback; **Birthdate:** 12.01.61
College: Wisconsin; **Height:** 6–2; **Weight:** 194; **NFL Years:** 2

		PASSING						
Year	Club	Att.	Comp.	Yds.	Lg.	TDs	Int.	Rat.
1984	Green Bay	62	27	310	56	2	6	30.4
1985	Green Bay	74	39	552	38	2	4	63.6
Totals		**136**	**66**	**862**	**56**	**4**	**10**	**48.1**

WRIGHTMAN, Tim CHICAGO BEARS
Position: Tight End; **Birthdate:** 27 03.60
College: UCLA; **Height:** 6–3; **Weight:** 237; **NFL Years:** 1

		RECEIVING				
Year	Club	No.	Yds.	Avg.	Lg.	TDs
1985	Chicago	24	407	17 0	49	1
Totals		**24**	**407**	**17 0**	**49**	**1**

STEVE YOUNG   JIM ZORN

YOUNG, Glen CLEVELAND BROWNS
Position: Wide Receiver; **Birthdate:** 11.10.60
College: Mississippi State; **Height:** 6–2; **Weight:** 205; **NFL Years:** 3

		RECEIVING				
Year	Club	No.	Yds.	Avg.	Lg.	TDs
1983	Philadelphia	3	125	41.7	71t	1
1984	St.Lou.–Cle.	1	47	47 0	47	0
1985	Cleveland	5	111	22.2	45t	1
Totals		**9**	**283**	**31.4**	**71t**	**2**

YOUNG, Steve TAMPA BAY BUCCANEERS
Position: Quarterback; **Birthdate:** 11.10.61
College: Brigham Young; **Height:** 6–2; **Weight:** 200; **NFL Years:** 1

		PASSING					
Year	Club	Att.	Comp.	Yds.	Lg.	TDs	Int.	Rat.
1985	Tampa Bay	138	72	935	59	3	8	56.9
Totals		**138**	**72**	**935**	**59**	**3**	**8**	**56.9**

YOUNG, Tyrone NEW ORLEANS SAINTS
Position: Wide Receiver; **Birthdate:** 29.04.60
College: Florida; **Height:** 6–6; **Weight:** 192; **NFL Years:** 2

			RECEIVING			
Year	**Club**	**No.**	**Yds.**	**Avg.**	**Lg.**	**TDs**
1983	New Orleans	7	85	12.1	32	3
1984	New Orleans	29	597	20.6	74	3
1985	New Orleans			Did not play		
Totals		**36**	**682**	**18.9**	**74**	**6**

ZENDEJAS, Tony HOUSTON OILERS
Position: Placekicker; **Birthdate:** 15.03.60
College: Nevada-Reno; **Height:** 5–8; **Weight:** 160; **NFL Years:** 1

			SCORING				
Year	**Club**	**EPA**	**EPM**	**FGA**	**FGM**	**Lg.**	**Pts.**
1985	Houston	31	29	27	21	52	92
Totals		**31**	**29**	**27**	**21**	**52**	**92**

ZORN, Jim GREEN BAY PACKERS
Position: Quarterback; **Birthdate:** 05.10.53
College: Cal Poly-Pomona; **Height:** 6–2; **Weight:** 200; **NFL Years:** 10

				PASSING				
Year	**Club**	**Att.**	**Comp.**	**Yds.**	**Lg.**	**TDs**	**Int.**	**Rat.**
1976	Seattle	439	208	2,571	80t	12	27	49.2
1977	Seattle	251	104	1,687	82t	16	19	54.3
1978	Seattle	443	248	3,283	64	15	20	72.2
1979	Seattle	505	285	3,661	65t	20	18	77.6
1980	Seattle	488	276	3,346	67t	17	20	72.4
1981	Seattle	397	236	2,788	80t	13	9	82.3
1982	Seattle	245	126	1,540	50	7	11	62.1
1983	Seattle	205	103	1,166	43	7	7	64.8
1984	Seattle	17	7	80	21	0	2	16.4
1985	Green Bay	123	56	794	56t	4	6	57.4
Totals		**3,113**	**1,649**	**20,916**	**82t**	**111**	**139**	**67.5**